I0062753

A SOLUTION TO EMOTIONAL TRADING
AND THE BUY-AND-HOPE PORTFOLIO

ASSET REVESTING

HOW TO EXCLUSIVELY HOLD ASSETS RISING IN VALUE, PROFIT DURING BEAR MARKETS, AND CONTINUE BUILDING WEALTH IN RETIREMENT

CHRIS VERMEULEN & ASHLEY MULOCK

Copyright © 2023 Technical Traders Ltd.

ALL RIGHTS RESERVED

No part of this publication may be reproduced, stored in a retrieval system, or transmitted, in any form or by any means, electronic, mechanical, photocopying, recording, or otherwise, without the prior written permission of the publisher.

For more information and inquiries, address Technical Traders Ltd., PO Box 875, Thornbury, ON, N0H2P0, Canada, or email Support@TheTechnicalTraders.com.

DISCLAIMER: This material should not be considered investment advice. Technical Traders Ltd. and its staff are not registered investment advisors. Under no circumstances should any content from our books, websites, articles, videos, seminars or emails from Technical Traders Ltd. or its affiliates be used or interpreted as a recommendation to buy or sell any type of security. Our research is not tailored to the needs of any individual, so go talk with your investment advisor before making trading decisions.

Warning: There is a risk of loss in trading. It is the nature of commodity and securities trading that where there is the opportunity for profit, there is also the risk of loss. Trading securities involves a certain degree of risk, and it may not be suitable for all investors. Derivative transactions, including futures and forex, are complex and carry the risk of substantial losses. Past performance is not necessarily indicative of future results. It is important that you understand all the risks involved with trading and that you should only trade with risk capital. This information is for educational purposes only.

Mandatory CFTC Statement on Hypothetical Trades:

CFTC RULE 4.41 - HYPOTHETICAL OR SIMULATED PERFORMANCE RESULTS HAVE CERTAIN LIMITATIONS. UNLIKE AN ACTUAL PERFORMANCE RECORD, SIMULATED RESULTS DO NOT REPRESENT ACTUAL TRADING. ALSO, SINCE THE TRADES HAVE NOT BEEN EXECUTED, THE RESULTS MAY HAVE UNDER- OR-OVER COMPENSATED FOR THE IMPACT, IF ANY, OF CERTAIN MARKET FACTORS, SUCH AS LACK OF LIQUIDITY. SIMULATED TRADING PROGRAMS IN GENERAL ARE ALSO SUBJECT TO THE FACT THAT THEY ARE DESIGNED WITH THE BENEFIT OF HINDSIGHT. NO REPRESENTATION IS BEING MADE THAT ANY ACCOUNT WILL OR IS LIKELY TO ACHIEVE PROFIT OR LOSSES SIMILAR TO THOSE SHOWN

Price charts shown throughout the book are from the charting platforms eSignal.com, and TradingView.com

CONTENTS

CHAPTER 1
A DIFFERENT WAY TO INVEST

Do you wish you could spend more time doing the things you enjoy—travelling to exotic locations, hiking your favorite trails, biking along quiet roads, playing a round of golf, tending to your yard and gardens, or sinking into a good book?

Do you wish you had enough funds that you could spend more time with your family and friends?

Do you wish you could help your kids buy homes and start their own businesses, also leaving them an inheritance when you're gone?

Do you wish you were able to give money away to help others and never give it a second thought?

Do you wish you could do some or all of this without feeling guilty that you should be working or doing more to preserve your money and future?

Maybe you have tried to trade and invest your money for more growth and income, but these wishes still aren't coming true for you. Meanwhile, retirement is either looming on the horizon or has already arrived, and you feel in danger of running out of funds. You know something has to change if you're going to get where you want to be in life and make all these wishes come true.

What if I told you there's a different way to invest called ASSET REVESTING that, if followed, can help you make your wishes a reality?

You might be skeptical...as I might be reading a similar question. But even before it had a name or was a defined strategy, it turns out that the concept of asset revesting played a big role in getting me where I am now. Looking back from the perspective of what I know now, I have been practicing asset revesting for decades. It allowed me to build my waterfront dream home with cash at the age of twenty-seven. It has given my family a great life with the time and freedom to enjoy activities like kiteboarding, spearfishing, skiing, horseback riding, and traveling, to name a few. It has provided us with all the toys you can imagine—a private dock, jet skis, pool, and a cabana. And I get to share all of this with my family and friends.

My success with Asset Revesting has also given me the time and money to explore other business opportunities. I invented, patented, and licensed the world's first flying jet surfboard, getting government funding from the Scientific Research and Development Program in Canada. I also went on to help an electric vertical takeoff and landing aircraft company, which won a United States Department of Defense (DoD) funding award, and I became an equity owner in the company.

Real estate is another type of investment I'm passionate about. I own several rental properties and even built a self-storage facility for monthly recurring income.

My success allows me to support charities and causes I believe in, too. I'm one of the founding fathers of the group 100 Men Who Care. As of this writing, we have organized and run nine charity events. My company, team, and investing community played a big role in a Jack.org fundraiser for youth mental health. All told, we have helped raise more than

$240,000 for different organizations so far. I have been able to become a better community member and give back to the world. There is no better feeling than helping others and seeing big smiles on their faces.

As if all that wasn't already enough, the best part is what my soul connects with the most: the privilege of helping people like you learn how to use the same strategies with your money that I use with mine. I get to do and experience lots of incredible things simply by managing money in this more efficient way, and I get to help you do the same.

When you have all the success you could possibly want in this life, you don't "have" to do anything. Instead, you "get" to do whatever you want. What I "get" to do is spend my time helping you.

So without further ado. . .

HAVE YOU FALLEN PREY TO THESE COMMON INVESTMENT TRAPS?

If you're like most investors, you have probably spent years spinning your wheels, falling into one or more of these common traps:

You have FOMO (fear of missing out) on gains, and you allow your emotions to get in the way of your investment strategy. Typically, this problem results in severe drawdowns, losses, time wasted, and emotional stress. (If you don't know the term "drawdowns," don't worry—I will explain it in Chapter 4.)

You've followed stock trading newsletters, and when the trades didn't work out as expected you opted to jump from one strategy to another to another. This has only led you to become too aggressive, too angry, and too defensive when questioned about your success, or lack thereof.

You have no clear trading strategy or rules. You aren't sure when to buy or sell, you aren't using stops, and you struggle to follow a trading plan.

You believe that the only way to achieve above average returns is through high-risk investments and to always be in a trade.

You chase trades or investments that you hear about on the news, see posted on social media, or that drop in your lap from your neighbor who gave you a hot tip.

The investment strategies you used in your twenties and thirties are no longer viable because you don't have the time to recover from the kinds of losses those strategies generate.

You don't understand technical analysis well, you have trouble choosing stops and profit target prices, and you don't know how to identify market trends or reversals.

You have a financial advisor who is stuck in a diversified buy-and-hold and 60/40 portfolio mindset and who is not willing to change even though these methods are not working for you anymore.

Or . . .

You simply don't have the time or desire to learn about investing. You're just too busy.

If you identify with any of this, you're far from alone. **Short-term emotional trading and traditional passive investment methods are destroying the retirement plans of people just like you.** According to medical studies, this can cause enough stress to have a significant impact on your health. That just isn't okay.

There have been dozens of extensive studies in North America, Brazil, and Taiwan showing that 97 percent of all individuals who actively traded for 300 days or more lost money. And only 0.5 percent earned more than the initial salary of a bank teller—all with significant risk.[1]

It's pretty easy to see that if you don't want to end up in the same boat as most of the investors out there, you need a new method. You need a *different* investment strategy. And by different, I mean *not* what the majority is doing. You want to protect and grow your accounts, but you know the typical advisor can't do that with standardized strategies. So how do you do that on your own?

Buying into fads or stocks that spiked in price and performed well during a previous bull market, is not the answer. You need to understand and learn that buying what is going to perform for you in *today's* market conditions is a far more profitable tactic. It's this oppositional movement that will give you an edge over the majority and keep you from turning trading into a costly and emotionally devastating game.

Asset revesting will allow you to generate higher returns on your investments while minimizing risk. It can allow you to become financially free five, ten, or even twenty years sooner than the accepted "norm."

It can help you generate real growth and income for your retirement while protecting your capital and profiting from falling prices during bear markets. Imagine celebrating a bear market instead of fearing one...

In this book, I will provide a detailed overview of the Asset Revesting method. When you turn the last page, you will know how Asset Revesting works, different ways you can implement it, and more importantly, if it's something you want to use to reach your financial goals.

If you decide to become a Revester, you'll be able to ensure that your retirement is never again affected by market corrections and bear markets in stocks, bonds, commodities, currencies and more. You will understand how Asset Revesting can protect and grow your wealth in any market environment.

I will provide investor success stories and shed light on some hidden dangers and realities of investing that most people don't know about. These include types of drawdowns, sequence of returns risk, how the math changes as you near retirement and once you retire, and how you can make more money with lower annual returns. In short, you will learn how to generate more profit and income and have more free time with less stress and uncertainty.

Asset Revesting isn't an active trading strategy, and it isn't a passive buy-and-hold method. Instead, it's a style of investing between the two that uses common sense, logic, and both position and risk management, unlike all other methods. So if you are an active trader, this will feel refreshingly slow, simple, and low-risk, and if you are a passive buy-and-hold investor, this could feel a little more active than you are used to. Either way, it will be exciting to see your money protected and growing the way you know it should be.

THE BIRTH OF ASSET REVESTING

Looking back, the root of Asset revesting was born when the trading bug bit me at sixteen years old.

My father was a successful entrepreneur who was always inspirational to me. At the same time, I wasn't particularly excited about the prospect of working sixty to ninety hours a week like he did. So when, at the age of sixteen, I found an intriguing booklet by Larry Williams about how fortunes could be made from trading the futures market, I devoured it immediately. I was great with numbers, already loved the feeling of making money, and also loved the adventure of taking measured risks.

After reading the booklet several times, I asked my dad if we could start trading futures together. He was supportive but not interested. Fair enough. Nevertheless, I wasn't deterred. I still believed that trading might give me the perfect alternative route to making money and building wealth.

Coming from an entrepreneurial family, I was already primed for going my own way. I got my pilot's license at sixteen, allowing me to fly a plane before I could drive a car. Then, in college, I ran my own landscaping business every summer so that I could save money for trading.

In between classes, I was obsessed with watching the stock market on CNBC... and courting my future wife (but that's a story for a different book!). I wanted to learn everything I could. On the day I turned eighteen, I asked my dad to cosign a trading account with $2,000 I had saved over the summer. A week later, I was ready to rock and roll and began to trade from my dorm room!

Just a couple of months later, I turned $2,000 into $8,000, but from trading stocks rather than the futures I initially wanted to focus on. I stayed in school, earning my business diploma, specializing in business operations management. But trading was my true passion, and I was so successful at it that I eventually earned enough to pay for my final year of college.

After graduation, I continued applying my unique technical analysis skills to systemize processes, ultimately designing unique trading and investment opportunities that no one else was using. I always made sure each process included ways to manage portfolio risk through proper position sizing, as I had found that was paramount to success as a trader. I refined my processes and strategies over the decades and homed in on efficient asset allocation with low drawdowns, infrequent trades, and minimal risk. But don't get me wrong: There were some growing pains and some seriously hard lessons learned along the way.

For example, in 2001, I bought stocks that were growing their earnings by leaps and bounds. Unfortunately, when the dot-com bubble burst, my stock share values got cut in half and just kept Falling. I had to get out, and I took huge losses.

I realized that trading and investing methods based on fundamental analysis do not work in a bear market. I don't care how good the company is—even if it's the odd one that can buck a trend—it isn't worth the gamble. Like some of you reading this right now, I've blown up several trading accounts trying to be too aggressive with growth stocks and options.

Eventually, I pushed the limit even further to try to make my money back faster and moved into trading futures. Can you guess what happened next? Well, I blew that account up even quicker and lost more money than I ever thought possible. Honestly, it was in what felt like a nano-second. To say the least, it was an eye-opening experience.

After having lived through these learning experiences along with many bull and bear markets, I discovered that if you want to be a successful trader or investor, you must, as I have, navigate the markets differently from everyone else.

As you know, the challenges brought about from life lessons are enjoyed more when they are shared with others who also appreciate and value the insight. But to do so, and to be able to effectively talk about it, I needed to give a name to this life changing style of trading and investing. That is how the term "Asset Revesting" came to be.

There has never been a stock market more adept at separating people from their money. Nor have there ever been so many individuals near retirement or retired who must protect their capital and lifestyle. You and I both want the very best, so I am sharing Asset Revesting with you right here, right now, in this book.

THE PROBLEMS WITH TODAY'S MARKET

I'm going to be completely and uncomfortably open with you here: I'm generally a conservative guy. If you asked my wife, she'd tell you I was a laid-back introvert—and I am. But when I see something happening that just isn't right, and innocent people suffer as a result, it upsets me. And I want to stand up and help.

There is so much market manipulation now that the average investor and trader doesn't know what to believe or who to listen to anymore. If you have gotten sucked into hyped-up, high-risk growth stocks that have been *way* overvalued and then seen them crash 30 to 80 percent, taking you down with them, you have probably been given traditional financial advice, or been convinced by a stock trading newsletter promising you huge gains to buy and hold those positions. This has set you up with a portfolio of depreciated positions that you've been assured will eventually recover.

The problem is that you can't be sure they will recover. If you look at the past three bear markets, each has lasted an average of thirty-six months. When you account for the time to recover and recapture those missed gains, you're delaying your financial freedom and retirement by *nine years*. NINE YEARS! And this is only one example. There is no way to know ahead of time just how long the next bear market will last or how long recovery will take. Heck, the tech bubble took sixteen years to recover from. So the question becomes how long can you stand by, watching your retirement dreams slip away while downgrading your current lifestyle?

It doesn't need to be this way. You don't need to be an active and aggressive trader to generate big gains, and you don't have to spend your pre-retirement years desperately fighting to save every last penny so you can have some semblance of comfort when you do decide to retire. You don't have to spend your golden years constantly watching the markets and your portfolio statements, incessantly wondering and worrying if you'll outlive your money . . . or whether you'll be able to afford your current lifestyle in the years to come.

These common, yet very high-risk strategies, whether an aggressive stock or options trading newsletter or the volatile buy-and-hold method offered by so many financial advisors and institutions, can have a seriously negative effect on your investment account and lifestyle. I want to help you get out of these two extreme trading and investing strategies that the financial industry has brainwashed everyone into thinking they must follow, risking it all to get rich.

No more buying the hottest stocks, no more buy-and-hold, no more riding losses down, no more dollar-cost averaging, and no more diversification. What I'm going to show you will open your eyes to a whole new way to look at the markets and to protect and grow your capital going forward.

Asset revesting was a personal breakthrough when I first gave it a name. I felt that zing, that deep connection only the perfect word could illicit. I finally had a name to share with people for a style of investing that I *knew* would change the world.

Unlike traditional "investing," which is buying and holding assets long-term no matter what, this style of investing holds assets only until their upward trend reverses. Then, they are sold. The name Asset Revesting is descriptive: it reinvests capital into assets that are rising in value and doesn't hold onto assets that are falling.

It was a relief to me to have named an approach to investing that prioritized managing risk and aimed toward reaching retirement sooner. I felt empowered knowing that I could educate others about this investing style and help them avoid the pain of large losses and long recovery periods.

ARE YOU READY FOR SUCCESS?

The opposite of being a loser is being a winner. Asset revesting will turn you into a winner, but I want to make sure you're ready for that.

If you want to be successful, you must treat trading like a business, not a hobby, game, or sport. Investing is a serious responsibility that isn't a get-rich-quick vehicle and should never be treated as one.

So, what makes a trader successful? Not "accidenting" into profit by investing in a stock or index fund during a bull market. In fact, catching a lucky break with a big win is actually one of the worst things for an investor because it reinforces a false sense of reality and sets the wrong expectations.

Instead, trading success comes to those using asset revesting to (1) reduce risk and losses during periods of volatility and (2) trade actively and earn income and returns, even when the market is falling. As I always tell individuals, a boring strategy is a profitable one.

If you have been allowing the markets to carry you to success up until now, it's time to get serious and get some help because investing in your later years needs to be done very differently. The markets are quickly moving, turning confident traders and investors into confused and frustrated ones. I believe the perfect storm is brewing for baby boomers and retirees to experience a negative life-changing event. When it happens to their investments, it isn't going to be pretty. It is just a matter of time before the next financial reset happens.

If you don't want your portfolio and retirement to pay the price, you need to implement asset revesting today. It has been proven over decades through multiple market cycles to protect capital and allow for gains during bear markets and recessions.

After spending decades helping other traders and watching what's gone wrong in countless individual portfolios, I have come to understand that most traders need to focus on generating maximum growth while having strict capital preservation rules in place. This is the ultimate combination for consistent above-average returns without the stock market rollercoaster ride. It's only through this twofold method that you can survive bear markets and ensure the lifestyle you ultimately want.

This investment style will help you meet the objective of owning only assets that are rising in value, making it different from everyone else who buys and holds on for dear life to stocks, bonds, precious metals, crypto, etc. The buy and *hope* strategy (as I think of it) allows traditional investors to watch their assets fall sharply during market corrections and bear markets. Since holding onto assets as they plumet in value makes absolutely no logical sense, I only do two things now: follow price charts and manage positions and risk.

I'm not alone in using this strategy. I work with thousands of investors in 130 different countries. They range from billionaires to CEOs, advisors to retirees, pilots to engineers. The key to my system is to follow the rules just as pilots do when flying.

I truly believe that one of the reasons for my success as a trader and investor is my early experience as a pilot since it's all about checklists, rules, and systems. If I followed all that stuff, I found that I had fun flying, I was safe, and life went on. If I cut a corner or missed a step, I could die. So, I take procedures, steps, and systems very seriously, and that's how I attack the markets.

Coming back to my point, if you believe as I do that watching your wealth drop by 20 percent, 35 percent, 50 percent, or more by holding onto assets that are falling in value is a giant waste of time and money, we're on the same page.

Asset revesting is a simple but game-changing strategy that will give you more free time, help you make more money, and allow you to retire sooner. In fact, as you continue reading, you'll discover that if done correctly, asset revesting does the opposite of what you would expect in retirement. Instead of burning through your savings and slowly becoming poorer, you can actually become richer and live a more luxurious lifestyle than you ever thought possible.

Allow me, through this book, to provide you with the support and guidance to navigate yourself safely through turbulent market conditions and crush-raging bull markets to not only make it through safely but to always benefit and grow from market fluctuations.

I have always believed that people become more successful when they fully commit to an idea and process. I have devoted close to thirty years doing exactly that—living and breathing trading my entire adult life. I have traded all styles over the years from scalping to day trading, swing trading and long-term investing, fundamentals to technical analysis, stocks, options, currencies, futures, and ETFs. Through this experience, I have learned what works and what does not, and that's what I will share with you in these chapters. Let's go!

CHAPTER 2:
WHAT IS THE ASSET REVESTING STRATEGY?

ASSET REVESTING DEFINED

In the dictionary, "revest" is defined as "To invest (someone) again with power or ownership" or "To vest (power, for example) once again in a person or an agency."[1]

Here's my personal definition:

Revesting is the investor taking back the power and control of their capital for higher growth and preservation.

As a proactive investment strategy, asset revesting entails actively monitoring and adjusting the investments in a portfolio by selling assets that are no longer appreciating or are starting to decline.

The primary tool investors use with this method is an asset hierarchy, which is the order in which you value assets for potential return. For example, I believe the US stock market has the most potential to generate returns, so on my asset hierarchy, that would be the top asset class to own when the stock market is favorable. The next asset down my hierarchy

---

1   American Heritage ® Dictionary of the English Language, Fifth Edition. 2016 Houghton Mifflin Harcourt Publishing Company.

list with less volatility is long-term treasury bonds. The list of alternative assets within a hierarchy could include commodities, sectors, currencies, and more. It just depends on your preferences.

Using the hierarchy for positions is simple. If you own an asset that is lower on the hierarchy list when a top asset generates a revesting signal, you exit the lower position and enter the higher-ranked asset.

ASSET REVESTING STYLES

There are two ways to use asset revesting. The first way is multi-asset revesting, which means the strategy follows multiple different uncorrelated assets like stocks, bonds, currencies, commodities, etc., and uses an asset hierarchy to know which asset is best to own at any given time. Simply put, it rotates capital into the best asset for price appreciation or capital preservation, depending on the current market condition for maximum efficiency and risk control. This is my preferred trading and investing style.

In case you don't know the term "uncorrelated assets," let me quickly explain. They are often used in portfolio management to diversify risk. Uncorrelated assets are financial assets whose prices or values don't move in tandem with each other, meaning the performance of one has no direct effect on the performance of the other.

The second way to use asset revesting is the single-asset revesting method, which means the strategy only looks at and trades one asset. For example, if equities (SPY) are the preferred choice, a single-asset revester would only enter and exit that individual asset. When not invested in this asset, capital would remain in cash or a cash equivalent position earing interest or dividends.

Let's explore each of these strategies in more detail.

MULTI-ASSET REVESTING

As mentioned above, multi-asset revesting focuses on having a selection of uncorrelated assets, which are listed in what we call the asset hierarchy, and we rotate capital into the best asset for the current market condition. As a result, investors only hold assets that are rising in value, essentially gaining above-average returns while dramatically reducing portfolio volatility and drawdowns.

The asset hierarchy lists assets by their rank—with lower-risk, lower-return assets, such as treasury bonds and the dollar index, ranked lower than assets with higher-risk and return potential, such as the S&P 500 and Nasdaq. By limiting our trading to those on the asset hierarchy, capital is always allocated to the best-performing, highest-ranked asset.

For example, using my own asset hierarchy, if a high-ranking asset like the S&P 500 is trending downward, portfolio capital is invested in lower-ranked assets that are rising or generating interest income like treasury bonds, the dollar index, or potentially a cash position. But when the top-ranked asset generates a new revesting signal, the bond or dollar position must be closed, and the capital rotated into that higher-ranked position to maximize returns and reduce the risk of owning assets falling in value.

MULTI-ASSET REVESTING EXAMPLE

Here's an example of asset revesting that worked quite well during the market correction caused by COVID-19 that started February 24, 2020. We were able to generate additional profits for asset revesters who rotated out of the equities market and into long-term treasury bonds for a nine-day position, which rallied 19 percent while the stock market fell by over 30 percent.

After exiting the long-term treasury position, investors could have moved into the T-Bill bond ETF symbol BIL to collect dividends and keep their cash safe as they waited for an asset higher up in the asset hierarchy to stabilize and provide a new revesting signal. On April 20, 2020, the stock market generated a new asset revesting signal, and investors revested their capital back into the index ETF which at that point was priced 11 percent lower than where it had been sold just a month and a half earlier. This new index position went on to rally another 18 percent before generating an exit signal to move safely back to cash temporarily.

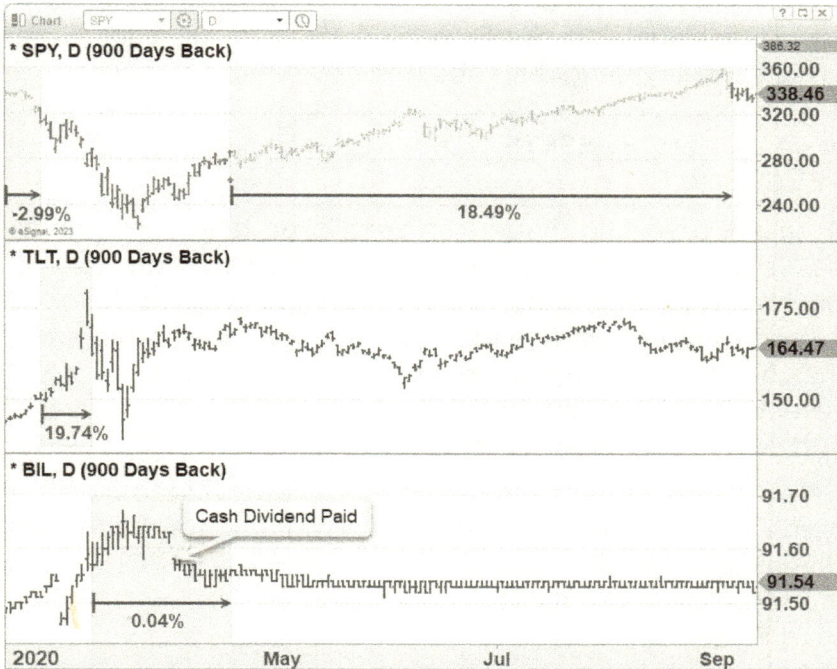

Figure 1

WHY SHOULD YOU CHOOSE MULTI-ASSET REVESTING?

Remember that in asset revesting, you can profit from a rising or falling market. This is achieved by tracking multiple uncorrelated assets, which means while some assets are falling in value, others will be rising. Because the strategy only holds assets that are rising in value, it provides a consistent opportunity for growth. Also, by adhering to a proven asset hierarchy list as I've said, you can substantially reduce drawdowns through positions with lower volatility.

If the financial market in general is extremely volatile and directionless, you will know how to take advantage of being in cash or cash equivalents. With my asset hierarchy, I do this by owning the US Dollar Index ETFs (either the long or inverse funds), BIL that earns dividends or literally by staying in cash while waiting for a low-risk, high-probability asset revesting signal. The question every revester must answer is: Which assets are right for you and your financial goals?

WHAT KIND OF ASSETS WORK FOR MULTI-ASSET REVESTING?

An asset revesting model can zero in on bonds, commodities, ETFs, and more. Since, like most investors, you probably hold a diverse array of investments in your portfolio, it's a pretty simple strategy to integrate. Whether the hierarchy includes stocks, bonds, commodities, or currencies, asset revesting requires two things: holding assets rising in value and selling ones that are in decline.

Now, here is a very important truth that I want to hammer home for you, and this is in general, not just for multi-asset revesting. Though you may love a certain stock, ETF, commodity, etc., just remember one thing - IT DOES NOT LOVE YOU BACK. Your favorite stock does not care that you have put all your money into its performance. Gold, silver, Bitcoin, etc, won't behave as you want just because you love them and think the market and economic climate favor that particular asset. If you can come to terms with this and know that, once sold, you can always buy these assets back at a later date when they are priced less and rising in value, you will be ahead of the vast majority of people trying to pull money out of the stock market.

Just like I will show you with single-asset revesting, it's important to carefully consider the pros and cons of this strategy before you decide if it's right for you.

PROS OF MULTI-ASSET REVESTING

- Helps to avoid prolonged periods of portfolio decline (drawdowns) by rotating capital into assets that are rising in value.

- Involves investing in noncorrelated positions, which can help reduce portfolio volatility.

- Offers more consistent and predictable portfolio growth.

- Has lower fees than other investment approaches by using low-cost ETFs vs. high cost mutual funds and does not require an advisor.

- Can be traded automatically in brokerage accounts.

- Helps reduce financial and emotional stress.

- Helps to protect and build wealth that can lead to the retirement you always envisioned.

CONS OF MULTI-ASSET REVESTING

- Requires a system to identify asset revesting signals.
- May underperform during extended bull market runs.
- Requires ongoing adjustment of targets and stops.

IS MULTI-ASSET REVESTING RIGHT FOR YOU?

Multi-asset revesting may be a good fit for you if you are seeking the following: (1) inflation protection, (2) asset preservation, (3) lower fees, (4) reduced sequence of returns risk, (5) lower drawdowns, (6) above-average returns (particularly during market corrections), and (7) a more predictable and rewarding investment experience.

You should carefully consider your financial goals, however, as well as your risk tolerance, investment objectives, and experience before deciding if this is the right strategy for you.

Without trying to make this sound like the holy grail or all-weather investment style, we truly believe multi-asset revesting is the best solution for younger investors because of the powerful compounding effect that can help them reach financial freedom decades sooner. Also, we believe it's the best option for investors who have accumulated a sizable nest egg they want to protect, while generating higher income from it each year, and who no longer have the time to recover from a multi-year bear market or recession.

If you're dissatisfied with your trading results or the limitations of traditional buy-and-hold/hope investing, you should seriously consider making the shift to multi-asset revesting.

VICTOR HAD JUST THREE YEARS TO MANDATORY RETIREMENT WHEN HE FINALLY FOUND MULTI-ASSET REVESTING

His extensive work hours as a short-haul pilot, sixty-two-year-old Victor didn't have the time or energy to invest, so he relied on his financial advisor to guide him.

Victor's days are long as he captains multiple flights, deals with weather delays, technical issues, and gate changes, leaving him with little energy after work. The FAA requires commercial pilots to retire by age sixty-five, so Victor wanted to start using his savings to build more wealth as soon as possible. His dream was to purchase a plot of rural land and start a small farm with crops and animals. He also wanted to make sure his children and grandchildren had an inheritance but didn't want his own lifestyle to suffer in order to ensure that.

Victor had read about something called swing trading, where he could take advantage of short-term changes in a stock's price, but he didn't understand how to analyze market movement. As a newbie investor, he underestimated the sheer volatility of the stock market, and when the COVID stock crash happened, he ended up panicking out near the market low. As a result, he lost 35 percent of his portfolio value, which held fast-moving growth and momentum stocks.

With only a few years left until his mandatory retirement, he was terrified. What did his future look like? Would he be forced to stay in the loud, crowded city, unable to buy the farm of his dreams? Would he be forced to take on another job after his "forced" retirement from aviation?

Swing trading hadn't worked, and since the buy-and-hold wasn't working either, Victor was going backwards rather than getting ahead. He had no time to lose, so he was determined to find a way to grow his portfolio regardless of whether the market was rising or falling. Another pilot told Victor about how his IRA performance improved during the 2020 downturn by following asset revesting signals. So, becoming curious, Victor began to do some research.

Deciding to go for it, Victor created an asset hierarchy that included some ETFs (including a T-Bill ETF) to put his cash in when nothing on the hierarchy was heading up.

Multi-asset revesting helped shield his portfolio from the market's worst downturns, as his assets were moved to cash or cash equivalents whenever stocks and/or bonds dropped. When the markets picked back up, he moved his assets to wherever they had the most potential for growth.

Over time, Victor's portfolio grew. He eventually followed the strategy with a larger portion of his investment capital. After a year and a half, he experienced firsthand how consistent and powerful investing can be with proper position and risk management in his portfolio. He was able to start enjoying life again versus worrying about running out of money before the end of it.

This different investment method transformed Victor's outlook and goal so that he is now well-prepared and excited about his mandatory retirement.

MULTI ASSET REVESTING KEY TAKEAWAYS:

- Rotating capital in and out of assets using an asset hierarchy.
- Protecting and growing capital by deploying position and risk management.

- May help to avoid prolonged periods of portfolio decline (drawdowns) through a system to identify asset revesting signals.

- May be deployed by anyone to help younger investors retire decades sooner or to help retirees who want to maintain their wealth and lifestyle.

SINGLE-ASSET REVESTING

Single-asset revesting focuses on moving in and out of a single asset or small group of closely related assets. This strategy provides reduced risk from the buy-and-hold method because it only owns the asset when price is rising. Therefore, it generates more consistent growth as your account is either rising with an asset or earning interest while waiting safely in cash:

SINGLE-ASSET REVESTING EXAMPLE

In Figure 2, you can see how the value of QQQ rises and falls over time. As a single-asset revester moving in and out of QQQ, you would make your entries and exits at each of the arrows, allowing you to take advantage of volatility instead of suffering because of it.

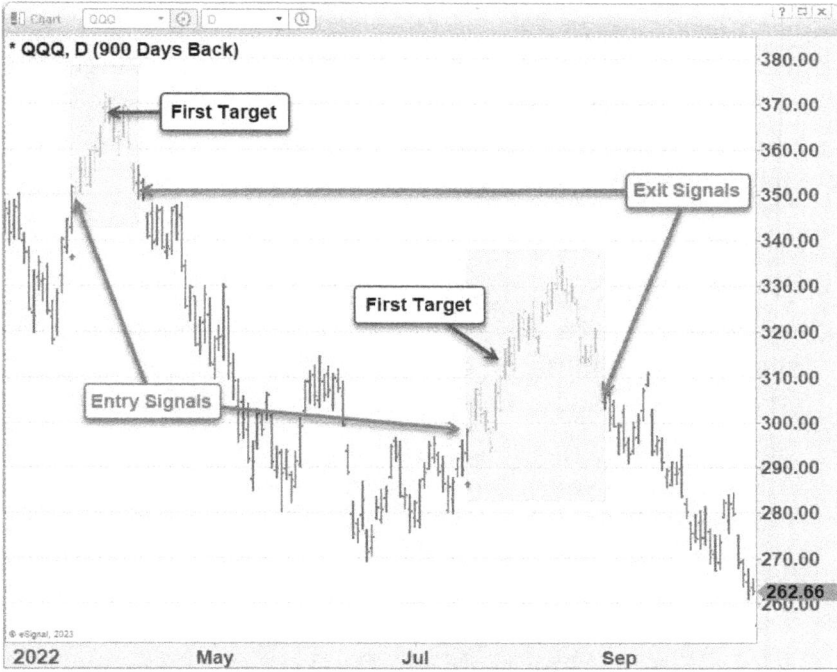

Figure 2

Single-asset revesting can be a useful approach for you if you have a high level of expertise, like particular assets, and want to focus your efforts on maximizing returns for one particular asset. This can include an index, sector, individual stock, bonds, commodities, currencies, or groups of related assets, such as precious metals like gold, silver, and miners.

Some proven single-asset revesting strategies and systems focus on trading ETFs, which provide maximum liquidity which is important if your account size is several hundred thousands of dollar or larger and don't want to deal with the headaches of scaling in and out of stock positions. ETFs are generally less volatile than individual stocks and trend more consistently.

Large amounts of capital can be invested with them at any given time, unlike stocks where the price can move with large trade orders and become costly when entering and exiting.

PROS OF SINGLE-ASSET REVESTING

- Potential for higher returns: By focusing on a single as-set or group of closely related assets (rather than a more diversified portfolio), you can more effectively identify and capitalize on favorable market conditions, potentially leading to higher returns.

- Ability to take advantage of short-term price fluctuations: Single-asset revesting involves actively trading an asset in order to take advantage of short-term price move-ments. This can be an effective way to generate returns in a relatively short timeframe.

- Simplicity: This is a simple strategy that involves focusing on a single asset or small group of related assets which move together. It can be easier to manage compared to a traditional diversified portfolio, which may require more time and effort to monitor, rebalance, and adjust positions.

CONS OF SINGLE-ASSET REVESTING

- Potential for missed opportunities: Single-asset revesting emphasizes a single asset or small group of assets that move together. By not following different, uncorrelated in-vestments, there is very little opportunity for growth when those related assets are falling or not moving higher.

- Requires a higher level of expertise: Single-asset revest-ing requires a higher level of knowledge and understand-ing of a particular asset in order to make informed de-cisions about when to buy and sell. If you don't have a strong understanding of the asset you consider revesting in, it may be more difficult to implement this strategy suc-cessfully.

IS SINGLE-ASSET REVESTING RIGHT FOR YOU?

Overall, single-asset revesting will be a useful strategy for you if you have a high level of expertise in a particular asset class, and you understand position and risk management. It can also be a powerful way to increase returns when you use it as part of your portfolio, as it provides diversification of investment strategies. One couple who benefited from integrating this strategy was Ed and his wife, Joan.

ED AND JOAN'S SINGLE-ASSET REVESTING JOURNEY

Ed and Joan are accountants. People often think that their work must only be busy in April and that the rest of the year, they can travel, sail, and golf. But that isn't how it works.

Their business is so busy that they rarely have time to enjoy any downtime. While April is certainly a high point with many clients submitting individual returns to the IRS, they have both corporate and personal clients who submit extension requests that move their filing dates to September and October, leading to an overwhelming influx of work late in the year.

Plus, Ed and Joan handle quarterly tax submissions and offer bookkeeping services year-round. In December, a time that's often spent with family, these two are busy helping clients plan last-minute tax-saving moves.

Because of their workload, they're often up before the sun and return home after sunset. Then, their weekends are spent catching up on paperwork and grabbing a moment here and there to see friends and the grandkids.

One of their shared passions is collecting antiques. Every room in their home has been meticulously appointed with beautiful pieces, many of which they hunted for years to find. While Ed and Joan would love to retire, they're concerned that their love of antiques, sailing, and travel will be too expensive to maintain without an income from their firm. Making matters worse, they were in the process of adding two small accessory dwelling units for guests to their hundred-acre property when COVID caused construction material and labor costs to skyrocket. So they've been left with half-finished, glorified sheds.

Ed and Joan have invested their money since their early twenties and have a very good understanding of how to manage their investments, routinely placing stops and limit orders in their brokerage accounts. In recent years, they've worked closely with their financial advisor, focusing on dividend stocks to help them generate an income that will allow them to retire. They also assume that the regular purchasing of certain dividend stocks will result in dollar-cost averaging that lowers their overall basis.

In the past, their portfolio usually kept pace with a typical 60/40 portfolio, but outperforming that benchmark wasn't anything to brag about—especially after COVID, when both bonds and stock prices declined. If anything, recent events and volatility have made their retirement look more and more faint as it drifts even farther away.

They wanted to accrue money steadily, shifting out of the high-risk, status quo reward method (diversified buy-and-hold) with something more reliable.

One day, a friend sent Joan a funny commercial about asset revesting, which she shared with Ed. Intrigued by the volatility-avoidant method, they thought using a single-asset model, strategically moving their capital in and out of S&P 500 ETF might help their assets grow more consistently than if they were left holding on to stocks or bonds.

While financial advisors sometimes suggest a dividend-focused approach, Ed and Joan had experienced maximum drawdowns of as much as 38 percent over the years. They were comforted by the knowledge that asset revesting portfolios don't ride positions down as price falls and that they have low max drawdowns through the use of position and risk management. Because asset revesting controls risk and keeps any losses small, they decided to have a portion of their investment capital use the strategy to diversify how their money was managed.

They followed an asset revesting signal newsletter and moved their capital in and out of S&P 500 ETF as new revesting signals suggested. Ultimately, they kept their capital in cash equivalents when there were no signals suitable for investing.

This allowed Joan and Ed to take more money out of their investments to put toward the additions to their property. They were able to finish the units and are planning to have their children and grandchildren visit each summer. The couple is looking forward to potentially retiring in five years and wish they had started using this capital-protected, high-return style of investing sooner. But they're happy they discovered it when they did.

SINGLE ASSET REVESTING KEY TAKEAWAYS:

- Focuses on trading in and out of a single asset (stock, bond, commodity, or currency).

- A simple way to take advantage of short-term price fluctuations, but could be waiting in cash more often for a new trade.

- Requires a higher level of expertise or have access to asset revesting signals.

- Can be deployed by anyone with a portion of their capital and for those with a shorter investment horizon.

MANAGING ASSET REVESTING POSITIONS

As you have learned so far, asset revesting requires the continual management of positions and risks. This is accomplished by setting targets and protective stops to remove capital and avoid losses while also locking in gains. A typical revesting strategy might include (1) a stop set at a chosen percentage below the entry price and (2) a profit target to sell a certain percentage of the position when the specific gain has been reached.

Figure 3

Symbol	Entry Date	Entry Price	Allocation	Targets	Exit Date
	July 20 2022	$298.73	100%		
			25%	5.0%	July 29 2022
			50%	10.0%	Aug 11 2022
QQQ			25%	15%	
				Trend Exit	Aug 22 2022
				Stop Price	

Figure 4

As you can see from the asset revesting trade in Figures 3 and 4, a net profit of 7.3 percent was generated. At the same time, the buy-and-hold strategy experienced a strong rally, followed by a more significant sell-off, resulting in a loss from the beginning of the first price bar on the chart to the last.

With multi-asset revesting, it's important to note that targets and stops are updated to maintain objective reward and risk levels to accommodate changes, such as market volatility, price momentum, and dividend payments. This style of investing requires you to get comfortable with cash as an investment position and opportunity.

This may seem different and overly cautious, but remember that this strategy should never result in any big losses or multi-year drawdowns. It's based on the belief that it's better to maintain your wealth and lifestyle during higher-risk market conditions than it is to own assets falling in value.

SUCCESSFUL ASSET REVESTING WITH "PHARE"

Here are five steps I use as my guiding light for investing. These will help you achieve the following goals of asset revesting: (1) reduce risk, (2) identify trends with technical analysis, (3) select the strongest trending asset, (4) avoid unnecessary market volatility by moving capital to lower-risk assets, and (5) generate a steady income from assets.

1. **P**rotect capital using position and risk management.

2. **H**old only assets rising in value.

3. **A**nalyze asset price trends within your hierarchy.

4. **R**otate capital using revesting rules and signals.

5. **E**xecute trades in your portfolio.

Now, you understand that following an asset hierarchy means (1) consistently reinvesting capital by selling a position that is no longer performing well and (2) reinvesting it into an asset that is either starting a new uptrend or is already rising in value. This helps you optimize the performance of your portfolio and manage risk by continuously aligning your investments with favorable market conditions.

But how do you recognize which assets in the hierarchy are beginning their climb in value? By creating or using asset revesting signals, which you'll learn more about in the next chapter.

Remember, this book is to introduce you to a different style of investing. It's up to you to decide if it's something you should implement. My aim is to provide you with a high-level overview and framework about what asset revesting and signals are, as well as the ways you can use them.

CHAPTER 3:
ASSET REVESTING SIGNALS

For decades, we have been told that trading and investing are simple. Buy low, sell high. That's it! Invest in something today, wait a while until it goes up, then sell. But how does the average investor know when the stocks, ETFs, and other investments they are considering are low enough or high enough to enter or exit?

The rise and fall of stock prices over time tells a story. Essentially, investment performance charts are signals showing the market's "temperature" around a particular investment. A stock that is rising, for example, is popular, being bought more than sold. One that is falling, on the other hand, is unpopular, being sold more than bought. Of course, all of that can change in an instant—and very often does.

Asset revesting signals, once deciphered, tell investors to take action and enter or exit a position based on technical analysis of the price charts and the asset hierarchy, which helps to manage portfolio volatility.

HOW DO ASSET REVESTING SIGNALS WORK?

Asset revesting signals provide clarity on market direction and risks while removing the guesswork from trading. Using them controls risk by allowing you to follow price trends, hold positions when assets are rising, and quickly exit underperforming positions to create dramatically lower volatility within your portfolio. When any rule has been triggered, you know to take action and enter or close indicated positions. Ultimately, these signals allow you to avoid big losses and multiyear drawdowns to outperform the average market returns over the long run.

Asset revesting strategies using ETF investing signals and similar indicators for other investment types provide a proven, repeatable process that introduces consistency, control, and capital preservation. As the signals are all based on rules rather than news, predictions, or emotions, financial stress is reduced in favor of a clearer path to a predictable outcome.

Capital preservation is vital for asset revesters because you cannot prioritize a short-term battle over the long-term war. Without your capital, you have no means to access the upside potential offered by asset revesting. To preserve your capital, you must:

- Cut losses and not hold on to positions falling in value.

- Own fewer positions to reduce diversification.

- Wait for quality trends and positions to present themselves.

- Use cash as one of the most powerful positions during specific market conditions (extreme volatility, mixed bull/bear markets).

Interpreting the investment signals that markets are sending requires following proven research and trend analysis. Through these steps, you can recognize critical signals and better manage both risk and returns. It's an approach that can limit large losses while also helping you act on opportunities others might miss.

Asset revesting will allow you to focus strictly on signals that show price action to help put the odds in your favor. There are other benefits, too, as asset revesting signals:

- Works in any timeframe or market cycle.

- Works on any type of trading instrument (stocks, ETFs, options, futures, currencies, CFDs, and cryptocurrencies).

- Allows you to find low-risk and high-profitability trade set-ups.

- Allows you to define risk clearly and place protective stops and forecast prices several bars into the future (depending on the time frame used).

- Removes the guesswork from trading, allowing you to create a simple, repeatable system to generate profits from the market.

- Gives you clarity on market direction and risks, allowing you to focus on the important things while ignoring news and opinions. They reduce noise so that you can properly execute your trading strategy like a robot.

Sounds great, right? Well, it is, but before you can start putting it into play in your portfolio, you need to understand how these signals are interpreted.

HOW ARE ASSET REVESTING SIGNALS GENERATED?

The signals followed in asset revesting are relatively simple.

As discussed, when a held asset stops rising, and the price becomes bearish or weak, it creates a signal to exit. An asset that is rising in value triggers a signal to enter.

But what fuels the signals themselves? Where do the signals come from. The answer is simple, even if the process is complex. Asset revesting signals are generated through technical analysis.

By using technical analysis as the cornerstone of the asset revesting method, you reduce risk by following price trends and riding the coattails of the market. It's a widely held belief that a trend is more likely to continue than it is to change direction, and this strategy takes full advantage of assets when they are trending.

THE BENEFITS AND DRAWBACKS OF ASSET REVESTING TECHNICAL ANALYSIS

Let's get the drawback out of the way first. Asset revesting with technical analysis can, and sometimes, does underperform during market rallies. In general, a strategy that enters and exits positions to avoid large losses or which moves into leading assets will underperform in the short term.

You see, when you want to protect your positions and capital, it's important to trade and invest defensively. Trading is no different from defensive driving in a car, where we constantly scan intersections, check our mirrors, and look around to see where we are, where we are headed, and what is around us. Asset revesting ensures you are constantly scanning the market and related markets, checking price action to see where it's been and where it's headed, ultimately identifying what price patterns are forming (bullish/bearish).

This method is ideal for investors who want to preserve their capital and profit from bear markets, know when a new trend is starting, have inflation protection, have lower fees, have reduced sequence of returns risk, have lower drawdowns, and avoid running out of money in retirement.

But here's the rub. Asset revesting generally underperforms in the short run because it follows price action. By following price and waiting for trends to confirm before taking action, asset revesters tend to enter shortly after price has rallied and has been moving up long enough to confirm a new uptrend. Once the uptrend rules have been satisfied, a trade signal is generated.

It is important to note that as price rises, the strategy scales out of the position to lock in profits and reduce risk. But by doing this, when the market has a strong rally without any pullbacks or corrections the revesters will temporarily underperform and not generate the same return as someone who is using the buy-and-hole strategy.

Once price has completed its rally/move higher, it will eventually correct and start a new downtrend. When this downtrend is confirmed, another trade signals is generated to exit the position and a different position entered in another asset which is rising in value. As asset revesters, we are focused on identifying, confirming, and exploiting trends—not trying to pick bottoms or tops.

This means that while the asset revester is able to avoid big losses and/or drawdowns, their moves may not generate the same return as the stock index over a short period of time when comparing the stock index performance to the same index ETF position that strategy takes. But there are some simple methods to keep up and outperform during strong market rallies, such as trading a portion of the capital with a little leverage, or trading a faster-moving index like the Nasdaq, which is something I apply to my asset revesting strategy.

One of the places where asset revesting really shines is during a bear market. It's especially critical then because it provides a clear signal for each trade prior to entering and exiting, essentially putting the odds in your favor. It works on any type of trading instrument and any timeframe. If you like the income provided by dividends, asset revesting can take that a step further by showing you where to place your protective stop order. It can also show you when to take partial profits on the first sizable surge in your favor so you own dividend-paying investments when they are rising and are safely sitting in cash when they are falling. (Of course, I will go into more detail about the dangers of holding dividend stocks in a later chapter.)

Embracing this trading philosophy reduces emotions and downside risk, while increasing the number of winning positions you will make.

In the following chart, we look back to 2022. The ETFs, such as UUP, and XLE, as part of an asset revesting hierarchy, far outperformed the -18.34% loss in the S&P 500. These are the moves you can make when you know where to put your money during even the most turbulent times.

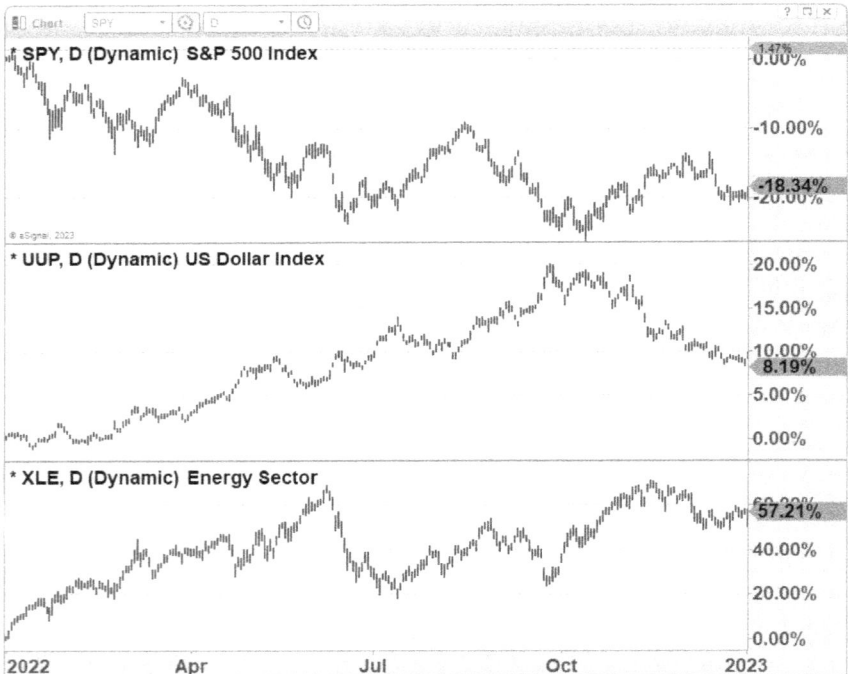

Figure 5

A bear market makes many investors feel like they only have two choices:

1. Close their eyes and hope for the best, while trying to minimize capital withdrawals.

2. Take a stab in the dark at when they should enter and exit various positions.

Asset revesting gives you a third bear market option: stem losses and create gains even while the stock and bond markets are plunging.

CHAPTER 4:
REAL-WORLD EXAMPLES OF ASSET REVESTING

One of the most frequently suggested investment approaches is the buy-and-hold strategy. This is the process of buying a "strong," possibly blue-chip stock and then ignoring market volatility and simply holding the position for a very long time, assuming it'll be worth more when you sell than when you bought. Essentially, this means holding a stagnant basket of assets during all market conditions, including corrections.

Sure, it can work to invest in positions over the long term and avoid active management of your portfolio, allowing the market to "do its thing," especially during a bull market. But with increasing volatility and more frequent market downturns, buy-and-hold is, at best, inefficient. At worst, it's a great way to run out of money early—especially thanks to drawdowns.

THE FACTS ABOUT DRAWDOWNS

Recently, I was shocked after speaking with a handful of investors on the phone. These investors have been involved in the markets for many years, and trade their own accounts. Shockingly, not a single one of them knew what a drawdown was. I have since discovered that it's a term few people know. This is a matter of concern for me as understanding drawdowns is vital to the results you can experience with your trading and investing. It is vital.

In short, a drawdown is how we gauge an overall investment strategy's risk level so that you know if a given approach fits within your risk tolerance.

A drawdown measures how much an investment or trading account is down from its highest point. It's used to quantify the extent of loss suffered by an investor or trader during a period of market decline. It's expressed as a percentage, and the maximum drawdown (MaxDD) is the largest percentage drop from the account's highest point to its lowest point over the life of the strategy. In layman's terms, it's the largest loss.

In addition to this value-type drawdown, there is a second type of drawdown related to time. More specifically, it's *the time it takes to recover from the value drawdown*. When you experience a significant drawdown, the years it takes for your account to recover to its previous level can delay or destroy your retirement plans.

Drawdowns can significantly impact your financial health, your physical and mental health, and your retirement lifestyle. It can take years to recover from large drawdowns (which are frequently experienced by buy-and-hold investors) and the stress, anxiety, and gut-wrenching fear experienced daily by those watching the destruction of their money and dreams is palpable.

Figure 6 shows these two types of drawdowns, which occurred during the 2021 market peak and 2022 market when using the typical diversified buy-and-hold stock/bond portfolio.

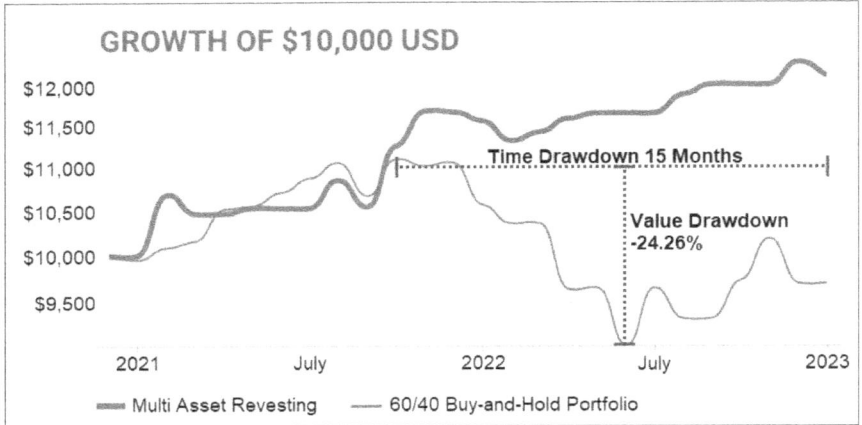

Figure 6

The graph represents the cumulative performance of a hypothetical $10,000 investment compounded. Returns don't reflect dividend income, the payment of any brokerage commissions, brokerage costs incurred as a result of buying or selling shares, and don't reflect the deduction of taxes.

One of the things investors often don't realize is that when you lose a large amount of money during a value drawdown, it requires a much larger gain to fully recover. Also, if you suffer a fifteen-month time drawdown, it requires *twice* that time to recover because you missed out on the gains during that drawdown term/timeframe. Plus, you need to earn the missed gains, which delays and pushes your retirement further out. As you can see, drawdowns cut twice as deep as most investors realize.

As we now know, drawdowns from a buy-and-hold approach create a high risk situation because the strategy is vulnerable to large drawdowns. In addition, the time it takes to recover often exceeds the time you planned to continue working to make money.

Figure 7 shows a perfect example of how traditional investors who buy and hold blue chip stocks and focus on dividends can suffer from large value drawdowns and massive recovery time drawdowns.

I would recommend taking a few minutes to really examine Figure 7 so that you can better understand what is at stake when using the buy and hold strategy. For example, what were you thinking, feeling, and doing from 2000 to 2013 when your investments were suffering?

Figure 7

Figure 8 shows an even scarier scenario. Unfortunately, most investors are lured toward riskier (aka sexier) assets, such as tech or biotech stocks, which are also known as "growth stocks." The issue with buying and holding these types of companies during a bear market is that they fall the most and take the longest to recover. But because they are called growth stocks, most investors think they are the best investments.

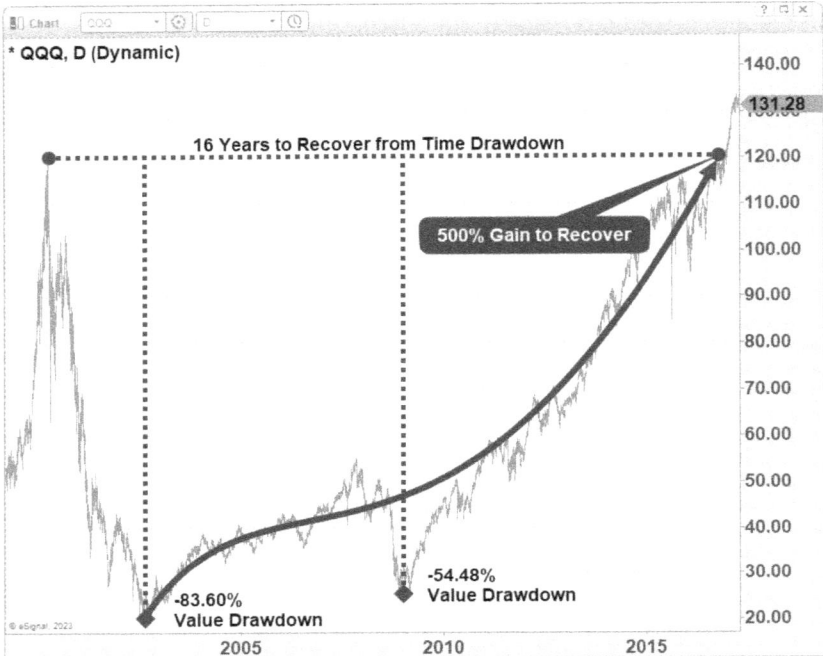

Figure 8

THE MATH OF WEALTH

Now that I have shocked your brain with some pretty scary numbers, get ready to be amazed by how different the lives of two pilots turned out after they each invested $1,000,000 for retirement and took out $50,000 per year to help pay for their lifestyles. You won't believe the stark contrast in their results!

As I mentioned earlier, investing math changes in your later years when how you invest is much more critical. It isn't about how much return you can generate each year. Instead, it's all about low volatility and consistency. This change in focus and expectation can take a bit of adjustment so don't be surprised if you feel a little discomfort during the process.

Let's look at the results of two different types of investors. First there's John, who used an asset revesting portfolio over the course of ten years that offered consistent returns, but averaged only 6 percent annually. Second, there's Mike, who used a more volatile strategy that generated an 8 percent average annual return.

As you can see in Figure 9, when it came time to sell shares to generate cash to fund their retirement, John ended up with more money than Mike, even though John earned a lower average rate of return. This is because John's portfolio was designed to minimize potential losses, while Mike's was designed to maximize potential gains. Therefore, it required Mike to sell more shares when the market dipped.

John: $1,000,000 Consistent Investor				Mike: $1,000,000 Aggressive Trader			
Year	Withdrawal	Return	Y/E Value	Year	Withdrawal	Return	Y/E Value
2013	$50,000	8.00%	$1,076,000	2013	$50,000	-14.00%	$817,000
2014	$50,000	6.00%	$1,087,560	2014	$50,000	7.00%	$820,690
2015	$50,000	7.00%	$1,113,689	2015	$50,000	-20.00%	$616,552
2016	$50,000	12.00%	$1,197,332	2016	$50,000	2.00%	$577,883
2017	$50,000	-5.00%	$1,087,465	2017	$50,000	35.00%	$712,642
2018	$50,000	6.00%	$1,102,713	2018	$50,000	-25.00%	$496,982
2019	$50,000	11.00%	$1,174,012	2019	$50,000	35.00%	$603,425
2020	$50,000	-3.00%	$1,088,791	2020	$50,000	43.00%	$791,398
2021	$50,000	13.00%	$1,180,334	2021	$50,000	16.00%	$860,022
2022	$50,000	5.00%	$1,189,351	2022	$50,000	1.00%	$818,122
AVERAGE RETURN		6.00%		AVERAGE RETURN		8.00%	

Figure 9

John, the consistent investor, became wealthier in retirement, while Mike became poorer. The crazy thing here, is that Mike earned a much higher average annual return than John, yet he was poorer. This happened because of something called sequence of returns risk, which is caused by selling shares during market corrections when the price is in a drawdown. I will explain shortly.

I call this *wealth math*, which is all about protecting our retirement accounts from losses and long periods of no growth. The annual returns may be lower than more aggressive strategies, but investments aligned with wealth math are a more consistent way to build wealth and generate income. At the end of the day, less is more for retirees, and average annual return is not as important as consistency.

Making more money and being able to live a more luxurious lifestyle with a lower annual return surprises almost everyone.

It's important to review your portfolio's investment strategy at each stage of your life to ensure that you aren't taking too much risk. Doing this can help you avoid losing money and experiencing unnecessary stress. Based on our experience of talking to countless people, nearly all investors nearing retirement have their money invested in a much higher risk strategy than they realize.

HOW YOUNG INVESTORS RUIN RETIREMENTS

Let me share with you a story about Mark, one of my clients, who was a fifty-nine-year-old retiree looking to secure his portfolio. He had experienced market volatility before, which caused him to have a lot of sleepless nights. He came to us for a more conservative way to manage his investments. After he reviewed our investing strategies to find out which one fit his financial goals and risk tolerance, and after he did the recommended personality test, he decided to use our multi-asset revesting newsletter signals. He felt that this strategy would help him feel more secure and avoid market volatility, while producing nearly two times higher annual returns than what he was currently getting with his advisor.

However, just a few weeks later, Mark called to tell us that his son, who was a financial enthusiast, had convinced him to take a more aggressive approach with a different service. Despite our warnings about the potential risks, he followed his son's advice, and what happened next is likely exactly what you are thinking. The market ended up declining, causing Mark to lose a significant amount of money from his portfolio.

Now, is there anything wrong with listening to the advice of well-meaning people? No, of course not. But in this case, both Mark and his son forgot to account for the fact that Mark no longer had the luxury of years to recover from a market correction.

Unfortunately, I see this all the time. A younger investor and even some far more experienced ones fall for an aggressive strategy that trades all the fast-moving stocks at a high level of risk. The issue is that everything is good until it isn't, and when the drawdowns build, the investor quickly finds out the strategy is far riskier than they wanted. But by the time they realize it, the damage has been done.

SEQUENCE OF RETURNS RISK

How many times have you heard someone refer to cash in your portfolio as a waste because it's missing out on opportunities? After all, if your cash isn't actively invested, it isn't working for you, right? Nope.

Just like any investment, cash is a position. It plays an important role in your hierarchy as a hedge against having to sell assets for liquidity during a bear market and also as a hedge against falling stock and bond prices—or both. It also protects you against something called sequence of returns risk.

THE CASH-STRAPPED PORTFOLIO

One of the most damaging things a retiree can do is liquidate stocks at the wrong time. Let's say you have 100 shares of Company A and 100 shares of Company B (Figure 10). If Company A is priced at $100 per share, you have to liquidate ten shares to get $1,000. This leaves you with ninety shares participating in any rise in the stock's value. If Company B is $200 per share, you only have to liquidate five shares to get that same $1,000, leaving you with ninety-five shares participating in rising stock prices.

Company A: 100 shares $100 p/s	Company B 100 shares $200 p/s
Liquidating 10 shares	Liquidating 5 shares
$1000	$1000
90 shares	**95 shares**

Figure 10

Now, imagine you need to withdraw another $1,000, but the price of Company A has fallen to $50 per share (Figure 11). You now need to liquidate twenty shares to get your withdrawal, leaving you with just seventy shares participating in the upside potential. If, at the same time, Company B's share price has risen to $250 per share, you need only liquidate four shares, leaving you with ninety-one shares.

Company A: 90 shares $50 p/s	Company B: 95 shares $250 p/s
Liquidating 20 shares	Liquidating 4 shares
$1000	$1000
70 shares	**91 shares**

Figure 11

When depressed assets are liquidated early in retirement to meet income needs, the amount of remaining shares that can participate in any market recovery is reduced. Over a short amount of time with repetitive liquidations, especially in a bear market, you will run out of money far sooner than you expected. This risk increases when you refuse to consider cash a position during price corrections and bear markets.

EMBRACING CASH

The lowest position on an asset hierarchy is cash, but it is still a position. Naturally, asset revesting portfolios rotate to this position as market conditions change, and you manage risk by locking in partial profits as positions and asset trends mature and reverse direction.

There is an ETF for this as well (BIL), which is a one-to three-month T-Note. It's just like a cash position, the difference being that monthly dividend income can be generated while your portfolio waits for new opportunities.

To avoid sequence of returns risk, it's critical to sidestep the bear market and take advantage of asset revesting signals to exit positions and move to cash within your portfolio.

As mentioned before, withdrawing funds when a portfolio is in a drawdown can be very costly to your long-term financial outlook. But with asset revesting, a strategy should never have any big losses or multiyear drawdowns. That means your portfolio will generally be near a high watermark (all-time high), leaving you free to use capital as needed.

DANGERS OF DIVERSIFICATION

It's common for an advisor to promote the diversification angle in a buy-and-hold portfolio, as it has been hailed as the holy grail of investing. They will tell you that spreading your capital out through different investment vehicles, industries, countries, and sectors will help you hedge against risks. But as billionaire investor Warren Buffett says, "Diversification makes very little sense for those who know what they are doing."

In reality, diversification is often used to camouflage that your money is being spread like peanut butter across different kinds of stocks and assets. What this does is provide you with a false sense of security by reducing your average annual returns and helping protect stockbrokers and advisors from getting sued for making bad investment choices. When one stock or asset begins to fall, a nonfiduciary-bound advisor can easily say something along the lines of "but look at what's happening over here" and distract you from what can potentially become a huge loss.

If the traditional buy-and-hold diversification strategy is being used, and you are nearing retirement or already retired, it's again up to you to ask and find out the maximum drawdown of the strategy. I have found that no one cares about your money as much as you do, so if you don't take the time to learn a little about how it's invested, you'll be destined for subpar results like everyone else. It's your money, so you need to become an advocate for it and for yourself.

A NEW APPROACH — HARVEY AND BETH'S JOURNEY

Every week, I hear from clients whose lives have changed thanks to asset revesting. By and large, most of them had either adopted an active/aggressive trading strategy or worked with traditional advisors to use the buy-and-hold (i.e., buy-and-hope) strategy. As a result, they watched years of hard work and savings vanish during market downturns.

One of those clients, Harvey, was seventy-four and had worked hard all his life for a large, multinational company to support his family and save for a comfortable retirement with his wife Beth. The two of them loved traveling with their friends, spoiling their grandchildren, playing pickleball, boating, and having weekly card games.

When they sought out the services of an advisor, who could help them manage their investments in the early 2000s, they did their homework and even got referrals from friends and their CPA. They went with an advisor they felt understood their situation and who had worked with clients with similar goals and needs. They were excited to have a plan in place so that they could focus on retiring at sixty-five.

Their advisor went for diversified investments across a wide spectrum of asset classes of stocks and bonds. He rebalanced their portfolio periodically, selling off positions that had done well and adding to positions that had underperformed in order to bring the 60/40 (stock/bond) allocations of the portfolio back into their target ranges. This is a seemingly logical approach that's used by virtually every financial firm.

Like many other investors, Harvey and Beth's portfolio imploded during the 2008 bear market, which forced them to downgrade their lifestyle and delay their retirement plans by six years. Needless to say, they were worried. Would their investments keep fluctuating in value? When could they realistically retire?

The aftermath of the 2008 bear market also did a lot of damage to their psyche, which still lingers today. They lost all trust in their advisor for not helping them protect their capital and preserve their retirement. And worse, they lost a lot of confidence in themselves.

By now, you understand wealth math and drawdowns enough to clearly see how this approach hurt Harvey and Beth. Realizing that due to the stress and anxiety their losses produced, they may not be healthy or fit enough to go on some of the adventures they planned was devastating.

When they came across asset revesting, they did their due diligence homework and decided to give it a try. This time, they were able to avoid and even profit from the bear market in 2022, pushing their retirement accounts to new highs as stocks and bonds fell. They were able to control the volatility within their portfolio, which is simply crucial for retirement. The byproduct of managing risks and positions also yielded greater returns. Harvey and Beth sidestepped market corrections and bear markets while the typical portfolio fluctuated 34 percent or more during the 2022 bear market. They actually made money during an otherwise terrible year for investments across the board.

As a result of using the asset revesting strategy in 2022, they were able to set money aside for a dream vacation they never thought they'd be able to afford and make a contribution to a college fund for their grandchildren. More importantly, Harvey and Beth gained confidence in their ability to invest that they had never had when someone else managed their money. Once again, they felt secure about their financial future with their first adventure bought and paid for.

FROM BULLISH BONDS TO BEARISH

The stock market isn't the only market that's been bullish in recent years. Few investors today remember the bond market before its forty-year bull run. The very idea of bonds going into bear territory is so outlandish that many investors and advisors are standing by the traditional wisdom of the 60/40 portfolio and continuing to increase bond holdings as you age, which only amplifies the risk.

Yet, let's look at the ten-year treasury rate over the past forty years. One quick glance shows the rate trending down. In fact, from 2010 to 2022, the rate chart formed a bottoming pattern and then clearly reversed and started to rise. As rates rise, bonds fall, and this could be just the beginning of a new major multiyear trend.

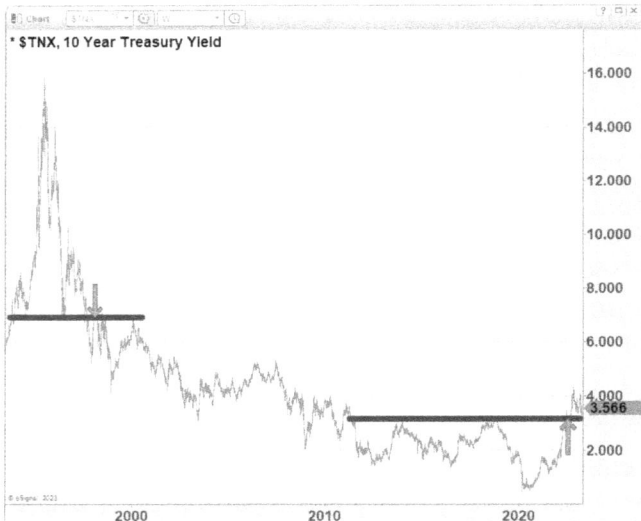

Figure 12

Bonds are not the conservative inflation-beating move they once were. You might think they are at least better than keeping part of your portfolio in cash, but as you'll see in the next section, that isn't always the case. To illustrate this point, let me introduce you to Alice.

TRADITIONAL ADVICE — ALICES' EXPERIENCE

A sixty-seven-year-old retired schoolteacher, Alice always had a vested interest in her personal finances, but they plummeted after her husband Randall's death. She became depressed and struggled to find the motivation to maintain her portfolio. Instead, she spent her days reading novels and consuming mindless television shows. As a result, cash started to get tight.

Alice went to a financial advisor at her local bank, who recommended laddered bonds, explaining that each one would have a different maturity date and interest rate. The further out the maturity date, the higher the interest rate. And because bonds have a guaranteed rate of return, she would profit regardless of market volatility.

In her haste to get this done and secure the bonds, Alice didn't consider how she would maintain her lifestyle in the meantime. She soon learned that she couldn't live off the bond interest rates alone. This meant that she would either have to downgrade her lifestyle or dip into her principal, neither of which was an appealing option.

Of course, she knew about the common investing strategies that her parents and husband had used. She also remembered the difficult years when recessions or market corrections happened. It took a long time to claw back what they lost and even longer to grow their accounts to previous highs and beyond. After allotting a couple of hours a day for research, Alice came across asset revesting, which she thought could work for her.

She liked the idea that rather than holding on to assets no matter what, assets decreasing in value were sold. If, later, their value began to increase, they could be bought back, and often at a lower price. This alone just seemed like good common sense.

Deciding to try it for a few months with a portion of her account that wasn't locked into bonds, Alice found that not only was her capital well preserved with the profit targets and protective stops she placed, but she could also generate an income to support her post-retirement lifestyle. As her confidence in the strategy grew and her bond contracts matured, she was able to allocate more funds to asset revesting. Eventually, she decided to sign up for the autotrading service in order to avoid the possibility of making mistakes herself. When her account started to grow without her having to place the trades, she finally knew asset revesting was exactly what she had hoped for when starting on this investment journey decades ago.

MOVING AWAY FROM THE 60/40 PORTFOLIO

When you look at the actual performance of bonds over the last twenty-five years, you can see volatility increasing with 15 to 20 percent swings becoming standard in recent years. While volatility can be good for returns, it can also gut a portfolio. Worse, the larger your losses, the higher future gains need to be to get you back on track.

Whether you're embracing the traditional stock/bond 60/40 approach, you go super conservative at 10/90, or you embrace a higher-risk approach with just 10 percent of your portfolio in bonds, you can expect your portfolio to underperform the S&P compared to prior years. You will also have to endure even more uncomfortable drawdowns—just as investors have during the last three bear markets.

Look at Figure 13. Here, you can see how three portfolios performed. It turns out whether they had just 10 percent or 90 percent in bonds, they all underperformed the S&P 500 while providing no significant downside protection during 2001, 2009, 2020, or 2022.

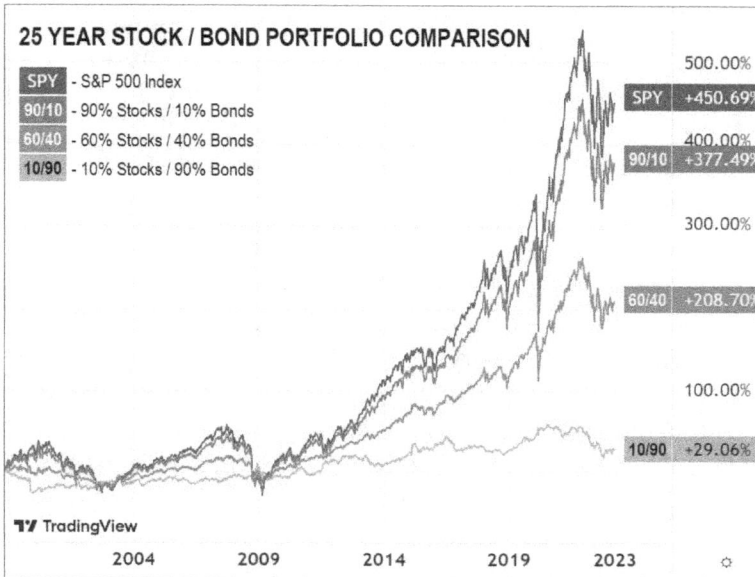

Figure 13

There definitely was a time when bonds—whether corporate, municipal, or treasury—were a conservative, defensive investment. Yet, in recent years, even treasury bonds have been increasingly shorted. According to fund managers responding to a Bank of America survey, their largest short positions in recent years have been US treasury bonds, creating downward-selling pressure on the asset's value as shorting investors position themselves to profit from a drop in value.[2]

After over a decade of pumping money into bonds through quantitative easing (QE), the Federal Reserve began unloading its accumulated assets in a process called quantitative tightening (QT).[3] No one knows exactly how QT will affect the broader bond market, but many expect interest rate volatility to increase.[4]

---

2   Randall, D. Analysis: U.S. bond investors worry deep slide will end 40-year bull market. Reuters. April 28, 2022. Accessed July 19, 2023. https://www.reuters.com/business/finance/us-bond-investors-worry-deep-slide-will-end-40-year-bull-market-2022-04-28/.
3   http://www.northerntrust.com/united-states/insights-research/2022/weekly-economic-commentary/unwind-quantitative-easing
4   http://www.ft.com/content/2496105a-d211-4abe-ab5d-46a91876428f

The signs of a weakening or strengthening economy are everywhere if you know where to look. The number of emerging market corporate bonds trading at 60 percent below face value increased over 300 percent back in 2022, and the amount of high-yield corporate bonds trading 30 percent below face value doubled.

Because of these extreme bond levels, the New York Fed created a new bond market distress index to help investors see early warning signs of bond market problems. Unfortunately, long-term treasury bonds had already fallen over 45 percent from 2020 to 2022, and high-yield corporate bonds had fallen as well. The most popular corporate bond ETFs, like HYG and LQD, had followed suit, losing substantial value, making the new bond market distress index not very useful to individuals up to that point. This is because most of the damage was likely already done to the bond market and investor portfolios.

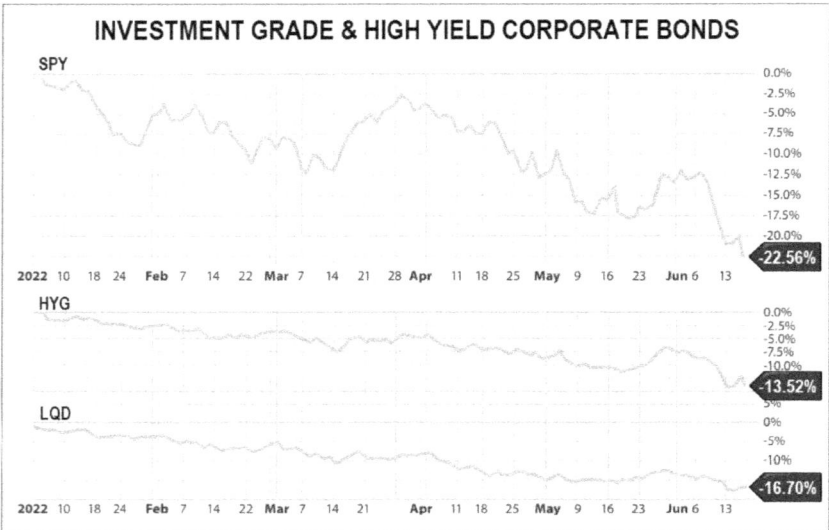

Figure 14

This isn't just something that has happened in recent years either. Bonds have sold off with stocks during the 2001 and 2008 bear markets. Mind you, the drop in value was not as substantial as in more recent years. And take a look at the downward trajectory of the same bond-focused ETFs during the 2020 COVID crash (Figure 15). Not very many people expected the price of stocks and bonds to plummet in value together. This caught most investors and advisors off guard.

But tactical investors who follow price trends and implement asset revesting have been able to identify these trends and profit from them in a very controlled and consistent way.

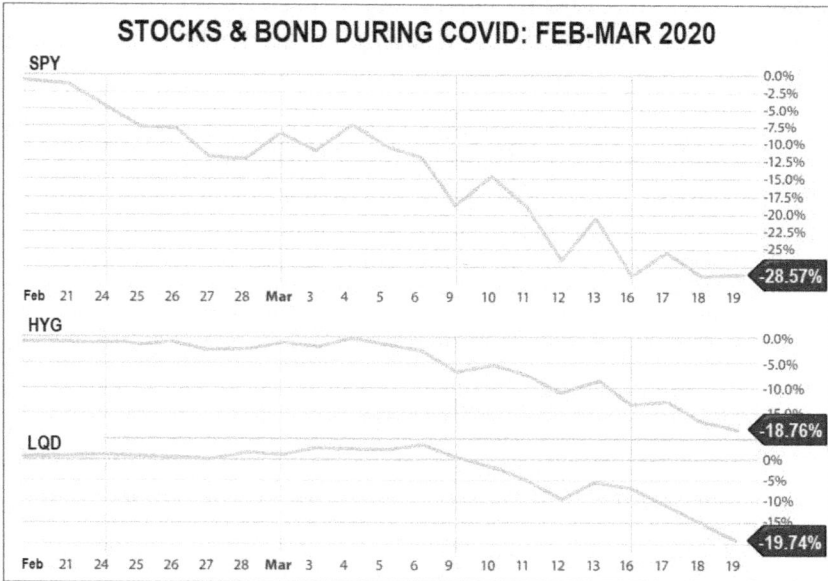

Figure 15

But what about dividend stocks? Aren't they a great way to protect your assets *and* bring in an income during a bear market or in times of great volatility? I hate to burst your bubble, but like so many common investment assumptions, this is an inefficient, dangerous idea. Let's explore it in more detail.

THE DIVIDEND DIVIDE — BENJAMIN'S CAUTIONARY TALE

Over the course of thirty years, sixty-eight-year-old retired entrepreneur Benjamin built his restaurant into a chain spanning the New England region. Two years ago, he sold the company to spend more time with his wife Nancy, their three children, and their five (and counting) grandchildren.

Unfortunately, Benjamin's health was quickly worsening due to the physical toll of working in his restaurant for so many years. Carrying heavy ingredients, cooking, and standing on his feet for hours every day caused permanent injuries in his feet, ankles, and knees.

He wanted nothing more than to spend his remaining years relaxing, birdwatching, walking through the woods surrounding his lovely Vermont home, enjoying barbecues with his family, and passing on his love of food and nature to his grandchildren.

Financially, his sole goal was to enjoy his retirement without spending so much that he had nothing to leave behind. His son Gary referred him to a financial advisor to help his money grow. The advisor recommended dividend stocks and told him to reinvest the dividends so that dollar-cost averaging would improve his cost basis and increase his gains.

Investors like Benjamin are often told that dividend stocks are the Hail Mary pass of investing.

When explaining why, many advisors discuss how dividend reinvestment creates a perfect environment for dollar-cost averaging, especially during a bear market.

Dollar-cost averaging through dividend reinvestment occurs when dividends are not taken in cash but are instead used to purchase additional shares at the market price, impacting the overall cost basis for the holding. But a reduced cost basis wasn't going to help Benjamin reach his savings and investing goals. What would help, however, was asset appreciation.

Even if a dividend stock is outperforming the S&P 500, think about it: isn't that a terrible benchmark in a bear market? What a low bar it is to have your assets outperform an index that's losing value! When you have large portfolio holdings in both utility and blue chip, high-dividend-paying stocks, your portfolio may temporarily outperform the S&P 500 index during a bear market, but keep in mind that it is still dropping in value.

If dividend stocks are dramatically outperforming the benchmark during a bear market, all that means is that your portfolio will be down *less* than the benchmark while your assets will still fall in value. It can take years for your portfolio to recover from this. If you are nearing retirement or already retired like Benjamin, you don't have the luxury or time to simply "outperform" a losing benchmark.

As one of our clients put it, "Most financial advisors forget that the main reason they were hired was to make a profit for their customer and not to just lose less than the S&P 500."

Dollar-cost averaging through dividend reinvestment may sound great so that you can own more shares at a lower price of a stock. But it's nowhere near as effective as owning positions that are rising, or holding cash and collecting interest when all other assets are falling. But I digress, let's get back to Benjamin's story.

The losses Benjamin suffered from the various market setbacks far outweighed the advantages of dollar-cost averaging. He tried to hang on and wait out the drawdowns, but when his home needed significant repairs, he had to sell some of the dividend stocks and lock in those previously only paper losses. This exposed him to sequence of returns risk, as you read about earlier.

When Benjamin stumbled across asset revesting while watching YouTube videos one evening, he realized he might have found a viable alternative.

Upon learning about and deploying a multi-asset revesting strategy, he discovered that every few months, his investment account made new highs. It was an incredible differ-ence from the extreme volatility and drawdown of 16 percent that others experienced in 2022 with traditional investing methods. He no longer worried about what the remaining years would bring financially. With his growing assets, he knew his children would have plenty of money to upgrade their houses, and he could send his grandchildren to college or even help them start their own businesses after he passed away. And he could accomplish this regardless of whatever repairs his house or car needed in the meantime.

DITCHING DIVIDENDS

We look beyond dividend stocks to other areas if stocks nor bonds are not trending higher. As shown in Figure 16, the UUP Dollar Index ETF was the investment of choice in 2022. Both the stock market (SPY) and dividend stocks (SPYD) fell in value, while the Dollar Index (UUP) posted substantial gains with low volatility.

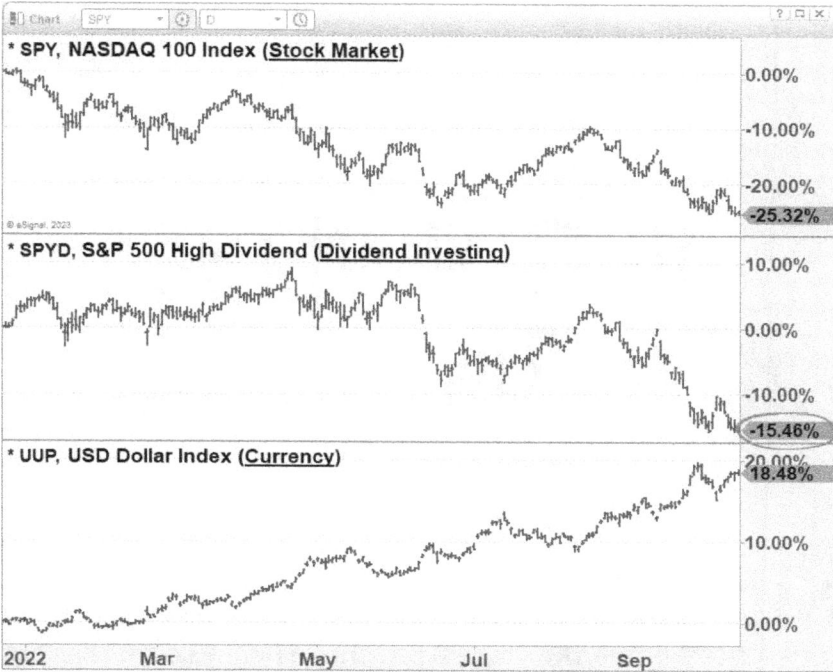

Figure 16

Dividends are a weak reward for holding on to a losing asset. When real bear market selling pressures take hold, blue chip stocks—including dividend stocks—sell off. The tactical play is to move into something with no correlation and less volatility during market uncertainty and falling stock prices if you want your investment accounts to grow continuously year after year.

CHAPTER 5:
GETTING IN THE REVESTING MINDSET

Many investors take actions that aren't in their best self-interest. They make irrational trades based on "tips" they've heard or strategies they saw in some random article or video, or because they love and use a company's product. They trade based on emotion rather than logic, allowing greed and fear to drive their decisions. They hold on to losing positions due to their unwillingness to admit they made a bad trade. Or they feel they're stuck in the trade because their position is down too much, so it isn't worth taking the loss. They think it's better to hold until it recovers. The list is endless, but those are the main killers. Beware!

On the other hand, successful traders—like asset revesters—all have a few things in common. Developing these characteristics and habits will help make you a successful asset revester, too.

1. **Asset revesters set goals.** Asset revesters tend to be incredibly goal-oriented. Why? Most people perform at their best when they reach for a clear goal. There are three basic qualities that make up a clear goal:

a. It must be realistic. If your goal is to make 25 percent or more every year, it isn't realistic.

b. It must be attainable. Just like with a realistic goal, an attainable one must be within your current capabilities. The best goals are short-term. Make your first one small and then increase them as your experience and skills improve. World-class sprinters don't think they can win the Olympics in their first year.

c. It must be measurable. Goals that aren't precise enough to be quantified or measured aren't really goals at all. If yours is to be wealthy, that's great. But what does *wealthy* mean to you? Our guess is that your definition of wealth will change as you get older and your net worth increases. If you can't define your goal and measure your progress toward it, you have no way of assessing your progress. Therefore, you can't make changes to your techniques and strategies that allow you to reach your goal.

2. **Asset revesters are confident they can reach their goals.** Confidence is a key to staying rational, logical, and disciplined. Starting with small, realistic goals will help build your confidence in yourself and your abilities.

3. **Asset revesters realize that success can come at any level.** Whether you're a beginning asset revester, one with some experience, or someone who makes his or her living strictly from trading, you can be successful. Many people think they have to have significant capital or years of experience to pull money out of the market consistently. That's not true. By the same token, if you don't stay disciplined, focused, and rational, you'll end up as a losing trader, regardless of your level of "expertise." All successful individuals started with small accounts. They didn't trade more than they could safely risk, and they learned from their mistakes. They developed a system that worked for them and fit their personal style. Regardless of the strategy they create or select to follow, it will be logical, rules-based, and will require self-discipline to execute it with success.

4. **Asset revesters specialize.** It simply isn't possible to understand and stay in touch with everything that occurs in all types of investment vehicles and markets. While some asset revesters have developed systems that allow them to trade in multiple venues (for instance, in different stock markets around the world), most of them specialize in a particular type of investment and particular market. You may enjoy trading stock indexes, growth stocks, or precious metals, for example. By focusing on trading assets you're passionate about, you will stay in touch with those assets and related events easier because it won't feel like work. Whatever you decide to specialize in, it should be your focus and where the majority of your trades take place. If you aren't interested in options trading, for example, don't trade them. Your lack of knowledge and motivation would only cause you to lose focus and make mistakes. Successful traders pick an area and gain in-depth knowledge of it, following it closely and learning from past trends and patterns, as well as from their own experiences. If you're a beginning trader, we recommend focusing narrowly on a particular investment vehicle and market. Learn all you can in that area, both about the market and about yourself, before you move into other investment types.

5. **Asset revesters take losses in stride.** No one likes to lose, but losing is a fact of life for investors. The key is to *limit your losses* and maximize your successes. A losing trade is not a failure. It isn't a reflection of you or of your overall skill. After all, if it was possible to be right every time, we'd all be rich. Some of the best traders in the world take astounding losses. Look at hedge funds in 2022. Despite hedge fund managers' experience and access to both information and technology, the global hedge fund index showed the sector down by more than 11 percent during the first bear market sell-off from the beginning of 2022 to September 2022.[5] The only way a losing trade is

---

5   https://portal.barclayhedge.com/cgi-bin/indices/displayHfIndex.cgi?indexCat=Barclay-Hedge-Fund-Indices&indexName=Barclay-Hedge-Fund-Index

truly a failure is if you aren't willing to take the loss without hesitation and move on to find a different asset rising in value. By accepting that you've made a losing trade and getting out of the position, you can focus on making money—not on being right all the time. Many traders feel they don't want to lose money on any trade, and they stay in positions in the hopes that it will recover to at least the break-even point. If you aren't willing to take small losses or don't have the discipline to take losses, you should not be trading. There are three problems with holding onto positions falling in value:

a. The position may never recover to the break-even point.

b. It ties up capital that could be placed into winning trades.

c. It's an example of unfocused trading and a lack of discipline, which would mean you aren't qualified to be trading. If this is you, accept it, or prove me wrong and take action!

6. **Asset revesters stay focused during rapid swings.** Most of us were raised to think that it takes years of hard work to acquire wealth. That viewpoint doesn't apply to investing in the markets. You can make thousands of dollars in days under the right circumstances. In fact, I once made more than $127,000 overnight in a single trade back when I messed around with penny stocks. Mind you, it was pure luck, and twenty-four years later, I have never experienced anything like it again. So don't count on luck! Asset revesters understand that money can be made or lost extremely quickly, and they stay calm and rational when that happens. Why is that attitude important? Let's say you've made several thousand dollars over the course of a month trading ETFs. If you allow your emotions to take over, and you begin to feel thrilled and excited, you may lose your composure and start making irrational trades. You may stay in the position longer than you should for one of two emotional reasons:

a. You think the market will keep going up, and you don't want to limit your gains.

b. You see the market fall, but you don't want to admit the market move could be over. So you hold on, hoping your position will rally.

    If you accept and understand that huge amounts of money can be made or lost in a short time period while investing, you are more likely to stay disciplined. I always tell investors that asset prices fall three to seven times faster than they rise. In other words, you can wipe out seven years of gains in one year if you are not careful. If that isn't a wake-up call, I don't know what is. Asset revesters take their gains in stride, no matter how large or small the gain may be. They quickly move to protect their positions by setting stops, which lock in profit on a portion of their position to reduce their risk and market exposure.

7. **Asset revesters are flexible.** Staying flexible requires that again, you stay detached and unemotional about your positions. No matter how strongly you feel about your position or a new trade, you have to be willing to change that opinion and act quickly, if necessary, when the analysis or rules require action. Asset revesters change their minds quickly and easily, and they are not concerned about whether they were "right" or "wrong." When it comes to trading and investing, detachment is your friend. The more flexible and liquid you are, the more successful you will be.

8. **Asset revesters realize that bad trades reduce the gains made from past trades and also affect potential gains from future trades.** Have you ever noticed that investors often tell you how much they've made while trading but never how much they've lost? It's like a scratch ticket player who gets excited about winning $10 on a ticket, ignoring the $100 they spent on losing tickets over the month. Successful investors are concerned with maximiz-

ing their gains and minimizing their losses. And to minimize losses, you have to acknowledge having had them.

9. **Asset revesters don't leap before they look.** One of the most common mistakes inexperienced investors make is to trade when they see an opportunity that they think might be too good to miss. Your personality plays a large part in this, and I'll talk more about this fear (FOMO) and how damaging it can be. But for now, I'll say this: Jumping into a position based on a hunch or on the belief that you may be missing an opportunity is no different than gambling. This is where mistakes are made and losses are maximized. Uphold your strategy, and follow your rules, no matter what. I believe it's better to potentially miss out on some gains than it is to suffer from a stupid emotional trade that wipes out a big chunk of your recent account growth.

10. **Asset revesters practice self-discipline, applying skill and logic to their trading.** They learn every day, and they use what they know to make intelligent decisions. They don't worry about missing out, take great pride in having a detailed plan to follow, and believe in their ability to execute it perfectly.

You may have noticed that a running theme throughout this list is not to allow emotions to take over. Since 1997, I've been trading and teaching others, and it's become crystal clear that I can provide investors with the proven strategy of asset revesting. It only requires them to follow the detailed trade alert signals I send out to build a large investment account to retire on. Unfortunately, many fail to follow along to the letter because their emotions and lack of self-discipline get in the way.

Fear and greed usually drive trading failures and are behind the instances where a trader can blow up their accounts. I know this is easy to do, because I blew up three trading accounts while learning how to manage risk when I first started.

According to the thousands of investors and traders I hear from, the number one issue they face is managing their emotions.

So that's the most important thing you can do to secure your trading success, including your fear of missing out (FOMO).

Let's take a deeper look at how emotions may be interfering with your trading success and how to stop that from happening.

HOW ANALYSIS PARALYSIS HURTS YOU

There's a fine line between action and inaction and understanding when to reposition your portfolio. One mistake some traders make is not doing anything at all. This is called *analysis paralysis* because it can paralyze you into a cycle of watching, waiting, and hoping.

This phenomenon occurs when you become so lost in the process of examining and evaluating various points of data that you can't make a decision. Imagine being a bullfighter paralyzed in the ring because you're unsure which way to turn. In seconds, the bull takes action and charges. If you wait, it's too late. Inaction can literally kill you as a bullfighter. As an investor, it means missed opportunities and can easily lead to losses. Unfortunately, this is the status quo situation that traditional diversified strategies offer.

Often, when examining a chart to decipher which way price will move next, the pros outweigh the cons or vice versa, the trader will have a clear direction and decision to make. When they succumb to analysis paralysis, it's usually because they feel they have to leave no stone unturned, or perhaps the pros and cons are equally weighted. The brain processes a plethora of information at once, and the human attached to that brain can get locked up.

Analysis paralysis is the trading version of information overload. Or it could be a personality trait of indecision that needs to be identified and overcome in order to be freed of inactivity. It's like writer's block, a fear of making the wrong decision, or any other inactive moment that causes lockup and results in a missed opportunity.

An investor can get overwhelmed by multiple scenarios and possibilities of movement in price. For example, if you try to follow too many technical indicators, some may contradict others, which is a common issue for those without a proven strategy.

If you read the opinions of others, which contradict each other, this can also lead to paralysis. The conflicting views create confusion and make it almost impossible to execute trades with clarity, discipline, and confidence. So you miss the good moves because you aren't quick enough to figure out your signal or because you're looking for more confirming indicators, even when you know the move is imminent. Thankfully, asset revesting provides you with a solution and makes investing easier and more predictable.

I had my fair share of analysis paralysis before I learned to keep things simple. I used to delve into all the details, putting together speculative theories that sounded great. But when it came down to pushing the button to execute a trade, I couldn't do it.

The information available on the internet to feed your thirst is literally endless. You can search, search, and search some more until your mind is frozen. The dividing line between useful and necessary analysis and *overanalysis* is a very fine one, however. Even asset revesters are susceptible to analysis overload.

So what is really going on here? Why do we feel the need to overanalyze our analysis? Could it be that the habit hides a major psychological issue? We think so. We think maybe it's a desire for control.

The search for information and confirmation fulfills a primal human desire in all of us: the need for certainty. No one likes to feel out of control, and the market can often make you feel that way because it can be uncertain and chaotic.

When the winds of change blow, the need for certainty can kick in and override the decision-making tools that serve you as an investor or trader. Uncertainty can make you prone to doing things you know deep down will not work for you. It makes you fear change, even if you logically know it will be a good change. And it's like being that bullfighter staring down the bull without taking action. You have to act, overcome the fear, and pull the trigger to adjust and manage your portfolio.

All the analysis in the world won't guarantee that you're on the right side of a trade. Overanalysis serves as a mental safety net that cocoons you in an illusion. You think you can predict with a higher degree of certainty the most likely outcome of an impending move in an investment.

There are only four things you can know for certain as an asset revester when you put on a new trade, no matter how much time you spend on analysis:

1. Your position size.
2. Your entry price.
3. Where your stop is.
4. Where your targets are.

Beyond that point, you are in unknown territory. Deep down, every trader, investor, and asset revester knows this, even though we try to override this deep truth with our research.

Of course, I'm not suggesting you abandon research and analysis entirely. They are critical to help you gain an edge. But they're just tools, not means to an end. Realize that spending hours on analysis actually stops you from making money.

Traders are often attracted to complex methods and systems. Complexity, however, introduces risks of over-optimization and curve-fitting. This makes systems and strategies sensitive to any change in volatility or market conditions and could become difficult to follow if there are too many moving parts and rules. Complexity isn't always better. I actually think that the simpler things are, the more profound they will be.

So choose the methods that make sense to you and that you are comfortable with. Use the methods you can learn or that you already know well. If you do this, trading opportunities will be clear, and you will be able to assess situations effectively, evaluate risks, and execute with conviction.

As Mark Zuckerberg said, "The trick isn't adding stuff; it's taking it away."[6] Nothing could be truer. If you want to be a winning trader consistently, you've got to take baby steps. Learn one area of the market at a time, and use only the best indicators and tools possible.

With that said, I also understand that not everyone has the time or desire to learn how to interpret market movement and convert it into trade signals, which is where asset revesting signal providers can be a time and portfolio saver.

YOU MIGHT HAVE STOCKHOLM SYNDROME

To some extent, inaction from analysis paralysis is worsened by a kind of Stockholm syndrome experienced by investors who believe financial advisors and firms when they are told that abnormal results are actually normal.

Traditionally, this term has been applied to hostages when they develop empathy for their captors. The hostages begin to identify with and even assist their captors. The most famous case was that of Patricia Hearst, a kidnapped newspaper heiress who was brainwashed during her captivity into robbing banks with her captors in the mid-1970s.

Investors can fall prey to their own version of this syndrome.

---

6   Taulli, T. From Under the Hoodie: 5 Entrepreneurial Lessons from Mark Zuckerberg. *Entrepreneur.* April 14, 2016. Accessed July 19, 2023. https://www.entrepreneur.com/living/from-under-the-hoodie-5-entre-   preneurial-lessons-from-mark/271229#:~:text='The%20trick%20isn't%20add-   ing,'&text=%22%5BThe%20proposed%20social%20networking%20platform,-   to%20work%20together%20with%20Zuckerberg.

ROGER'S STOCKHOLM EXPERIENCE

Roger was an investor interested in learning more about how I invest my capital. During our conversation, he told me about how he'd accumulated his million-dollar investment account while working a blue-collar job. He put away a few thousand dollars every year for thirty-plus years and followed the buy-and-hold strategy. He even asked his advisor to diversify his portfolio by picking some stocks he liked. It worked for him to build wealth because time was on his side, but it was far from sunshine and roses.

While the buy-and-hold worked during the first half of his life, it was challenging to weather bear markets along the way. For example, when stocks topped out in early 2000, his portfolio took over seven years to get back to even. During the bear market, he spoke with his advisor for investment advice. He was told: "Sit tight, ignore the falling prices, and you'll be fine if you hold through it." But the financial distress, sleepless nights, and relationship issues he had to endure when he was down more than 50 percent in only two years were a struggle, to say the least.

Roger then painfully watched his account claw its way back up for another five years, as the stock index reached its previous high. But the rollercoaster ride was far from over. Within a month of reaching a new high, the stock market collapsed again for another one and a half years. This was the 2008 global financial crisis in which he had to watch his investments fall more than 38 percent.

Once again, he called his advisor for support, but he was much more stressed and concerned this time. He was given the same advice, which cost him his marriage the first time around.

After thirteen painful years from the 2000 market top, the stock market returned to a new high in 2013. This poor man suffered a total of thirteen years with no growth and paid his advisor every year for this terrible, life-changing experience. And even though the stock market returned to the previous high, the investor was still down more than 15 percent because of the assets under management (AUM) fee (which I'll cover in more detail later in the book).

By 2020, Roger was in his fifties. He'd built substantial wealth through his dedication to saving and investing. He had a huge scare, but survived the 2020 COVID crash by holding on for dear life with his sage investment advice to "just hold on." In 2021, when he closed his eyes, he could see, feel, and smell his retirement, which was just a couple of years away.

But then, the unexpected happened. Both stocks and bonds plummeted in value. Like so many others like him, this pushed his retirement further into the future, and with inflation surging, he needed to downgrade his lifestyle and spending habits. All of this happened within the first few months of 2022.

His anxiety rose as he watched his wealth shrink week after week. Finally, he knew something had to be done because there was no way in hell he was going to postpone his retirement for another decade.

Once again, he called his advisor, desperate to protect his retirement. To his surprise, even after telling the advisor about his situation, wants, and needs, he was told yet again to just wait it out.

Understandably, Roger blew a gasket, fired his advisor, and in a panic, moved to cash until he could figure out what to do with his life savings. His online research led him to call me to learn more about asset revesting.

Roger had fallen prey to Stockholm Syndrome in two different ways. First, he believed that the best way to grow his savings was to have a professional manage it for him. If he'd had a really good financial advisor, then there would be nothing wrong with this. Roger, however, did not have a good advisor, he had a lazy one. Secondly, by trying to help his advisor add more stocks to buy-and-hold in his portfolio, Roger struggled to break free of the financial strategies that he was told to follow since saving his first penny.

People like Roger are so worried about missing out on a stock market rally that they are willing to expose themselves to big losses, sequence of returns risk, and delay, or even the risk of destroying their retirement. If this sounds like you, it's time to wake up and smell the hot coffee.

THE IMPORTANCE OF YOUR PERSONALITY TYPE

I share my Myers-Briggs personality results (INTJ) publicly for a couple of reasons. First, I enjoy sharing life experiences with others, including investors I work with. I believe in being open and honest with people and that I can learn something from everyone. Building a bond and trust with those who have similar passions and desires feels good all around.

Second, if you understand how people's brains work and how they think and react, including your own personality, you have a huge edge when trading and investing.

If you've never taken the Myers-Briggs personality test, or you haven't taken it recently, I recommend that you do. As long as you answer the questions truthfully, it will reflect the person you are now.

Here is a tip, try not to over think things when doing the test. Just read the question and pick the answer that jumps out at you quickly, then move on to the next question.

Each letter of the personality code indicates your personality preferences in four dimensions:

1. Where you focus your attention: Extraversion (E) or Introversion (I)

2. The way you take in information: Sensing (S) or Intuition (N)

3. How you make decisions: Thinking (T) or Feeling (F)

4. How you deal with the world: Judging (J) or Perceiving (P)

There are sixteen personality types, and the ones with the highest distribution are:

- ISFJ
- ESFJ
- ISTJ
- ISFP
- ESTJ
- ISTP
- ESTP
- ESFP

A common thread among these top personality types is the *S*, which stands for Sensing, versus *N* for Intuition. Sensing focuses on what you can detect with your five senses. Intuition focuses on the impressions and patterns gathered from information (data, technical analysis, chart patterns, statistics, logic, etc.).

As we know, the majority of traders lose money. A study showed after tracking 10,000 trading accounts for a year that more than half of them *lost* money during a one-year bull market rally. I believe emotions are the culprit.

Statistics show that 73.3 percent of individuals fall into the Sensing category, and if you know anything about the financial markets and how they move, it's all based on their emotional reactions.

Another reason we trade on emotions and get sucked into news and opinions is that stories sell ideas. If told well, they can trigger the senses in our brain to see, feel, smell, and even taste the things detailed in the story or news clip. Sensing personalities tend to follow stories that should be ignored, which is why I, as a technical trader, consider news to be useless, distracting, and potentially dangerous noise when it comes to trading and investing.

The second most common personality trait is Feeling at 59.8 percent, which falls under the Thinking or Feeling category and also plays a role in our success as investors.

THE DIFFERENCE BETWEEN THINKING AND FEELING

This pair describes how you make decisions. Thinking focuses on objective principles and impersonal facts. Feeling focuses on personal concerns and the people involved.

If you have an *F* in your personality type, you will likely be more emotional as an investor, which can lead to poor timing in your investment decisions.

Warning: If you have both an *S* and *F* in your results, I believe it's vital to embrace who you are and take action to create a plan, steps, and rules to follow when trading and investing. It's much easier for you to get sucked into news, opinions, stories, and hype, as well as feel constant FOMO, because it's just how your brain works.

If you know your results already and have either or both traits, don't panic! Being a Sensing and/or Feeling person is wonderful. And heck, I wish I had more of those personality traits because I'm the polar opposite. As I mentioned, I'm an INTJ, which means my personality type is more like the character Data on *Star Trek* who follows rules and uses logic to make decisions. That's an extreme example but a good reference.

Also, I should be clear that none of this has to do with your IQ or experience level. This personality test tells you how your brain is equipped to handle long-term thinking and the big picture.

In general, successful people are future-oriented and create goals and visions of where they *will* be someday. They think outside the box and dance to the beat of their own drum. These individuals are driven and follow their natural skills and passions, which for me happen to be stock market analysis and investing.

I deal with a lot of emotional people in my line of work—the good, the bad, and the ugly. But I understand what most are going through. Making or losing money and listening to strong news stories spark emotions, and they always will. It comes with the territory.

So take this quick test, figure out how your brain works, read your complete personality profile, and let it sink in. Be proud of who you are and what makes you unique. It doesn't matter which personality type you are. You can still reach financial success.

Here's the link to take the test: www.16personalities.com.

TRADING PSYCHOLOGY

If you've had any education in trading at all, you've heard that self-discipline is a major key to successful investing. I want to touch on this topic for a few moments to reinforce this point. Understanding the psychology of trading is the distinction between winners and losers.

Only you can be accountable for your actions. All the books, podcasts, videos, manuals, courses, or mentors can't give you self-discipline. It has to come from you. That's why it's called *self*-discipline!

This means that trading successfully requires an extraordinary amount of self-control and self-understanding. It requires the ability to quiet your mind when fear, greed, and other emotions creep into your decision-making process. You must have the discipline to step back and not trade when the situation goes against your feelings. It takes the desire to delve into your psyche and figure out what makes you do the things you do. It requires complete honesty and objectivity.

I have read a lot of trading books, and by far the most exciting ones have been about what other successful traders have done and are doing to build wealth. The *Market Wizards* books by Jack Schwager offer a thorough account of trading. He interviewed the world's most successful traders, and came to this conclusion:

"What sets these traders apart? Most people think that winning in the market has something to do with finding the secret formula. The truth is that the common denominator among the traders I interviewed had more to do with ATTITUDE than APPROACH."[7]

There are two aspects of investing psychology:

1. You must trust your trading method (in this case, asset revesting).

2. You must trust yourself.

It's obvious that to be a profitable trader, you need a viable trading method with setups, rules, and a plan that works. Without one, no amount of psychology will help you. Asset revesting is one such strategy.

The technical aspect of defining an investing method is academic. The psychological power to focus and remain disciplined is much more a matter of learning the techniques of spirituality and self-improvement. Both studies may sound contradictory, but they are the yin and yang of success in just about everything. Investing is no exception.

Knowing this is why I focus on helping those who have already been successful as an investor, professional, entrepreneur, or retiree. To be successful already, you must have drive, grit, focus, and be goal-oriented. It means with a little guidance, you already have the correct mindset, attitude, and self-discipline to become a successful investor.

At the end of the day, I want to be able to help everyone learn more about asset revesting and all the ways it can be used. But I cannot help those who won't help themselves first. I can't help those who see things only in black and white or right and wrong terms because this leaves no room for growth. I can't help those with a closed mindset, as there is

---

7   Minyanville. SPX Captures November's Markets; What's Next? *Nasdaq.* December 2, 2013. Accessed July 19, 2023. https://www.nasdaq.com/articles/spx-captures-novembers-targets- what-next-2013-12-02.

no room for possibility. And I can't help those who are addicted to the rush of trading—who would rather be glued to the computer screen all day and experience the elation and pain of market pops and drops rather than watch their account steadily grow. And that's okay. Asset revesting is not for everyone. Some aggressive traders have told me it's like watching paint dry. Some passive investors have told me that there is way too much action. If that's how they feel, that's fine, too.

EMOTIONS OF THE FOUR MARKET STAGES

Regardless of your personality type, you still run the risk of making decisions and trades based on emotion. In fact, these emotions are behind the four stages of the market and investments. Stan Weinstein coined them many years ago in his book Secrets for Profiting in Bull and Bear Markets, and I find they're a great way to identify market behavior and price characteristics:

- **STAGE 1, Accumulation**: The time when the volume of purchases increases.
- **STAGE 2, Markup**: The point at which buyers outnumber sellers and prices begin to rise.
- **STAGE 3, Distribution**: When the former buyers become sellers and stocks are being sold more than bought.
- **STAGE 4, Decline**: The point at which sellers outnumber buyers.

When a market or investment is in a basing stage 1, we know the price movement is driven by hope, while advancing stage 2 is driven by irrational exuberance and greed. The topping stage 3 represents a correction and top in prices, driven by the loss of optimism. This brings on fear and panic, both of which start the stage 4 decline where price is continually punished.

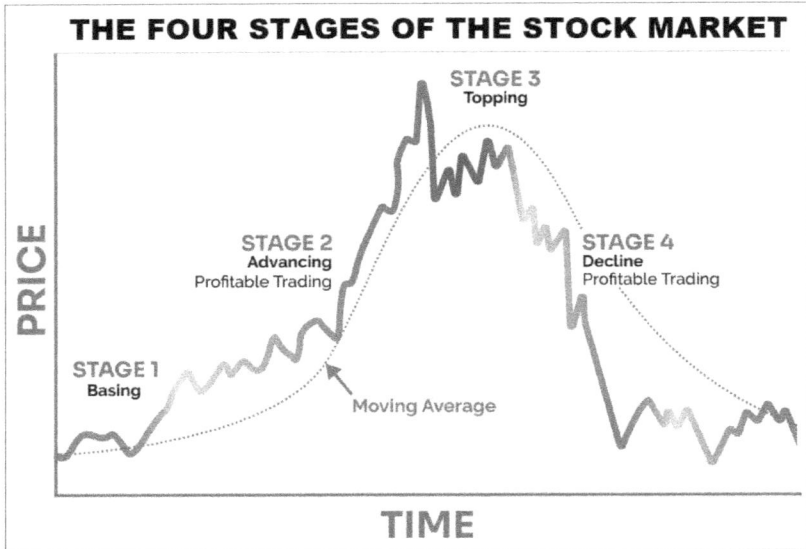

Figure 17

HOW TO RECOGNIZE STAGES

Recognition of each stage is paramount in trading, and here's how to do it.

The simplest way to identify the market stage is to use the 150-day simple moving average (Figure 17). Of course, you can get much more detailed in analyzing price, specifically using support/resistance levels, chart patterns, etc., but here are the core underlying rules to build upon:

Stage 1: Price fluctuates around the 150 SMA, which is relatively flat.

Stage 2: Price is consistently above the 150 SMA, sloping upwards.

Stage 3: Price is more volatile and fluctuates around the 150 SMA, which is relatively flat or rolling over.

Stage 4: Price is consistently below the 150 SMA, sloping downwards.

When we analyze market stages, we really are just analyzing the emotions of market participants who lack the skills and mindset to harness the markets. They can't see the forest for the trees. What's exciting is that knowing what we know, we can gain insight as to which stage the market is in, and depending how market participants are behaving, we can further gauge where in a stage the market is.

EMOTIONS OF THE MARKET

PRICE

EUPHORIA
I am a genius!
We're all going to be rich!

COMPLACENCY
We just need to cool off
for the next rally.

THRILL
I will buy more on margin.
Gotta tell everyone to buy!

ANXIETY
Why am I getting margin calls?
This dip is taking longer than expected.

BELIEF
Time to get fully invested.

DENIAL
My investments are with great companies.
They will come back.

OPTIMISM
This rally is real.

PANIC
Everyone is selling.
I need to get out!

DISBELIEF
This rally
will fail like
the others.

CAPITULATION
I can't afford to lose more.
I'm 100% out.

HOPE
A recovery
is possible.

DEPRESSION
My retirement money is lost.
How can we pay for all this new stuff?

TIME

Figure 18

As an outsider looking in, it can at times seem that markets are behaving "irrationally" and out of order. That's because undisciplined investors are falling victim to their emotions and losing control of their objectivity. As people behave irrationally, the market does, too.

Emotions can be regarded as a relentless opponent, often showing up without warning and striking us at inopportune times. As asset revesters, we are able to recognize their presence, maintain objectivity, and constantly assess our own strengths and weaknesses. There will ultimately be times where we can't control our own emotions, but we can always control how we respond to them.

Any time you recognize that your emotions are influencing your outlook, you're already one step ahead of the average market participant. It's at this point that you step back, refocus your perceptions, examine the price charts, and take the appropriate action.

An understanding of herd or mob mentality is important for both traders and investors. It can provide you with an edge over the average participant who doesn't contemplate what's happening around them. In a mob, we never know what the feelings and motivations are of all the individuals. There are, however, certain emotions that seem to appear at distinct times, and there is a certain predictability in their development.

An assets price action is no different. While we never know the underlying feelings and motivations of all participants, there are distinct emotions that are shared by the herd at various stages of an assets cycle. An understanding of these and their implications on the price is an advantage for savvy revesters.

All of this leads me to one final important point: successful investing and trading are boring. Yes, you heard me. The investors who think it's like watching paint dry aren't entirely wrong. But this is true of most things in life. Once you have mastered something and have a strategy, the process can feel relatively slow and dull. What this means is that you're in control of your money and emotions. But do you know what's never boring? Having more free time and money!

CHAPTER 6:

SELECTING YOUR ASSET REVESTING HIERARCHY

Asset revesters believe two things:

1. The way to protect capital is to own assets rising in value and to have stops in place to exit positions that are falling.

2. Analyzing and following asset price charts with technical analysis can show, with a high probability, when these positions are rising, range bound, or trending lower.

Of course, there are thousands of different stocks, bonds, ETFs, REITs, currencies, and other assets out there. Obviously, you can't track all of them in your asset revesting strategy, which is why you focus only on those you've chosen for your hierarchy.

UNDERSTANDING THE ASSET REVESTING HIERARCHY

As you've read, investors who decide to focus on a multi-asset revesting strategy require an asset hierarchy. For asset revesting to work, you must constantly monitor your chosen set of assets for trend change signals, indicating that it's time to move your capital from one asset to the other.

The hierarchy must function as a true ranking system, listing positions from high volatility (and high return potential) to low volatility. Additionally, each asset within the hierarchy should be a different type of asset with low correlation to each other.

When you're starting out, it's a good idea to focus on only one asset hierarchy and strategy. Your initial goal should focus on mastering the process of becoming a successful revester before adding more strategies and hierarchies.

Remember to have a positive mental attitude while on this journey. You must truly believe that you have the requisite abilities and skills to achieve your goals. If you believe in the back of your mind that your goals are unrealistic or that you don't have the ability to achieve them, you will succumb to self-doubt and will be more likely to give up. Whether you believe you can or you can't, you are correct.

Some of the different asset types are bonds, stocks, options, commodities, currency, real estate, and crypto, to name the most popular. Other types of investments, which are a little more unique and different, include annuities and collectibles like art, coins, diamonds, and antiques.

While there are many ways to own and invest in these varied asset types, the simplest and lowest-cost way is through the use of exchange-traded funds (ETFs), which is what I exclusively focus on as my investment vehicle of choice.

My asset hierarchy is based around the largest major assets—US stock indexes (S&P 500 and Nasdaq), twenty-plus-year US Treasury bonds, and the US Dollar Index. I like these because they are the most liquid assets, making it simple to move in and out of. They are assets we're comfortable with, and they provide us with opportunities to make money in almost all market conditions.

We can profit from a rising or falling stock market, and we can own bonds if they are performing better than stocks and have lower volatility. If the financial market in general is extremely volatile and directionless, we can take advantage of being in cash or owning a US Dollar Index ETF, either the long or inverse fund. This means it doesn't matter if the dollar is rising or falling—we can profit from the trend.

The assets in our hierarchy should have a low correlation between -0.30 to 0.30 based on the top asset in our hierarchy, which in this case is the SPY. This means the alternative assets on our list don't move in the same direction as the SPY. Also, we only own assets that are trending higher (bullish).

Last but not least, you will notice how each asset's daily volatility (price swing) becomes less as we work our way down the asset hierarchy. It's important because as the markets become wilder and have more risk, we move to lower-risk assets to counter the threat.

EVALUATING TRADING INSTRUMENTS

Your time horizon, risk tolerance, and overall familiarity will drive the investment vehicles you ultimately select for your asset revesting hierarchy.

For my asset hierarchy, the top assets for portfolio growth are US stocks. Decades of study have shown that the S&P 500 (SPY) and Nasdaq (QQQ) are the preferred indexes, providing the strongest long-term growth potential with the largest price fluctuations (volatility).

The stock market can have double-digit swings each year. If the US stock market is favorable and trending higher, it's the best asset to hold.

The next asset to focus on if stocks are *not* favorable are long-term treasury bonds (TLT). These can fall out of favor, however, and may not be a suitable investment just because stocks are falling. While this has caught many investors and advisors off guard, it doesn't surprise technical analysts who follow price.

What's nice about bonds is that they aren't generally as volatile as stocks. The hierarchy table in Figure 19 shows that

TLT moves a little less than what stocks move, which means investors can use bonds if they are favorable to protect capital better by holding a slower-moving asset that's rising in value during increased market volatility.

If neither stocks nor bonds are in favor, the next asset to look at within my asset revesting hierarchy is the US Dollar Index. Currencies generally have consistent trends and low volatility compared to stocks and bonds. Figure 19 shows that the Dollar Index (UUP) moves roughly 3.5 percent or half of what bonds move. Because the dollar has no correlation to stocks or bonds, and there is a long and inverse dollar index ETF, investors can move their money into whichever of these dollar ETFs are trending higher. This provides yet another way to consistently and slowly grow a portfolio during even the most difficult market conditions.

My Asset Hierarchy

Symbol	Correlation	Trend	20-Day Daily Percent Volatility
SPY	1.00	Bearish	2.45%
TLT	-0.10	Recovery	1.74%
UUP	-0.30	Bullish	0.71%
UDN	0.30	Bearish	0.75%
BIL	-0.20	Bearish	0.02%

Figure 19

Figure 20 shows what happens when we move money from SPY (US stocks) into TLT (bonds), then into BIL (T-bill/cash), then back into SPY. This illustrates how asset revesting position management works during a market downturn and how we tactically navigate assets for constant price appreciation.

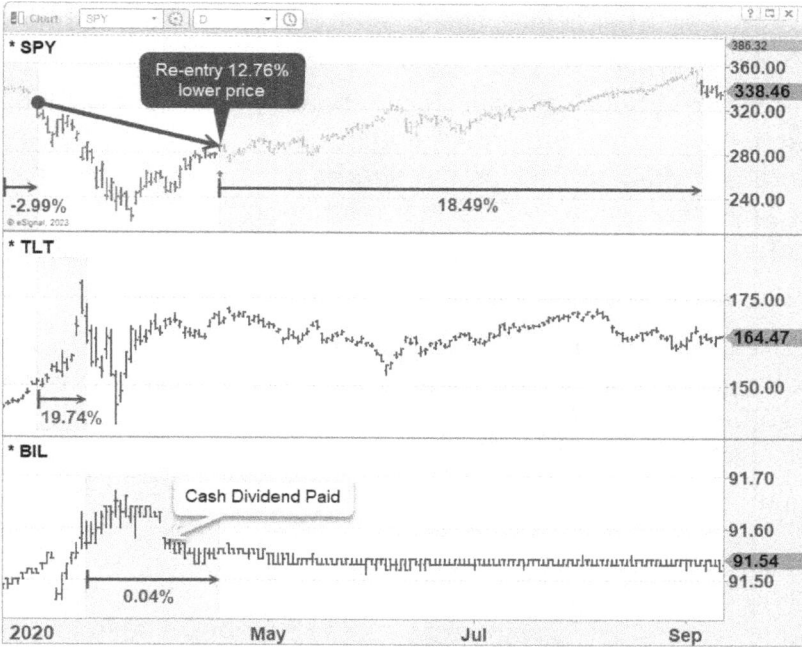

Figure 20

So the question is: Which assets are right for you? Again, it's critical that you choose the ones that you know and are comfortable owning, and you must have a strategy that works with your time horizon and risk tolerance.

My proven asset revesting systems focus on ETF trades because they are generally less volatile than individual stocks and trend more consistently. Also, large amounts of capital can be traded with them at any given time because of their liquidity. On the other hand, stocks can have large price swings with large orders and become costly when entering and exiting positions. I avoid this issue using ETFs. Let's take a moment to dive deeper into these:

- **Index Trading with Exchange-Traded Funds (ETFs)**

They are designed to mimic the price movement of a specific underlying index. These funds were created to provide the opportunity to trade the movement of an index like the

S&P 500 without having to trade the highly leveraged futures market or buy all 500 individual stocks.

For each share of the ETF purchased, you literally own a fractional share of the underlying equities of the index. These funds are easy to use, as the shares are traded like a stock (at any time without additional restriction) and can even be traded in pre- and post-market extended hours.

- **Leveraged ETFs**

There are leveraged ETFs available, giving you 1.5x, 2x, and 3x the percent move of the underlying asset. For example, if the S&P 500 or SPY ETF moves up 1 percent, and you bought the 3x leveraged fund, the leveraged ETF would move up roughly 3 percent. But these ETFs are not exact or perfect. They're a powerful tool for short-term, aggressive traders looking to profit from regular smaller moves. If you are managing a retirement account, however, I don't recommend using leveraged ETFs with large sums of money because they can do a lot of damage with one poorly managed position.

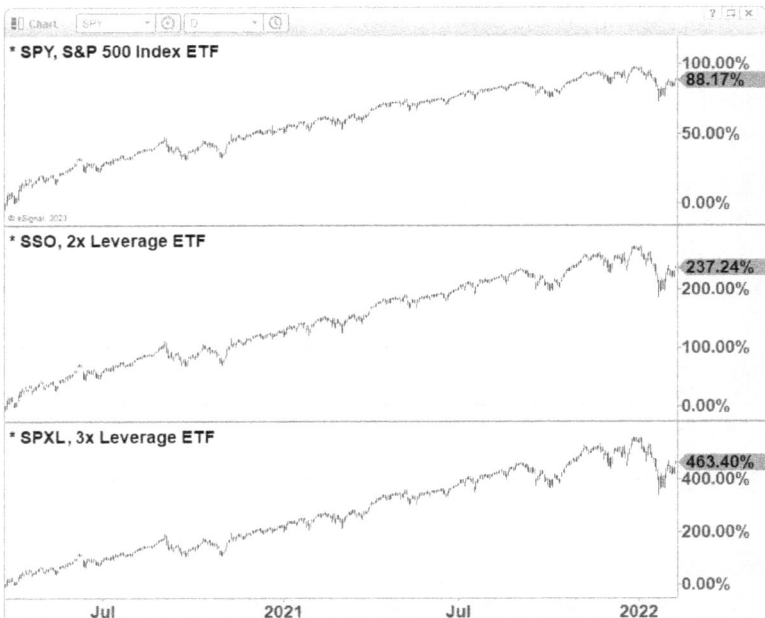

Figure 21

- **Inverse ETFs**

Many traders and investors don't like to short the market, meaning they borrow shares from their broker and sell them in the open market, hoping to buy them back at a lower price, return them to the broker, and pocket the difference in value for a profit. If you don't understand this concept, don't worry. There is no need for shorting anymore because there are now inverse ETFs, allowing you to profit from falling asset prices without having to take short positions. These ETFs move up in value as the underlying asset falls. All you do is buy an inverse fund (which are also available with 1.5x, 2x, and 3x leverage) and watch the ETF move higher in your favor as the underlying asset falls.

These ETFs follow the movement of the S&P 500 index, and as you can see, they move the same. The only difference is that the leveraged funds move in multiples of the underlying index.

Figure 22

Whichever group of assets you decide to put in your asset hierarchy, which can be non-stock market holdings like precious metals, crypto, real estate, etc., you have the power to control your risk and grow and build your wealth more consistently by rotating capital into only the strongest trending assets.

CHAPTER 7:
ASSET REVESTING ON AUTOPILOT

There are many obstacles that would-be traders and investors need to topple. For some, it's a lack of capital—which isn't something this book can help you with. For others, as we've discussed, it's their emotions. Some traders struggle with their focus and trading plan, which you should understand better by now after reading these chapters.

There are two obstacles that seem insurmountable, but for which I actually have a pretty simple solution. Those are the obstacles of human error and lack of availability. Depending on your lifestyle, you might not be available to execute trades when an asset hierarchy gives you a signal. Whether it's due to your work schedule, your sleep schedule, or your other commitments, you might not be able to enter or exit positions when needed.

Protective stop orders can help in that they limit the amount of losses you endure. Profit-taking limit orders allow you to manage investing pretty well no matter how busy you are. But what about the lost opportunities when you can't exit a position that's signaling an imminent downturn or enter a new position when the opportunity is there?

After helping individual investors navigate the markets for over twenty-five years, I've found the number one cause of failure is investors missing trades and mismanaging positions. This frustrating and seemingly impossible obstacle can easily be overcome when you use an automated system that executes all the trades and manages positions for you. Asset revesting strategies can be connected to an investing account and executed for you, completely hands-free. They can also work with regular self-directed brokerage accounts, IRAs, corporate accounts, joint accounts, trusts, and more.

This method is similar to how the popular robo-advisors like Wealthfront, Betterment, and others execute trades from a technology standpoint. The two main differences are that an autotraded asset revesting strategy doesn't use the old, diversified strategy like the robo-advisors do, and most providers of an asset revesting strategy don't have an costly asset under management (AUM) fee.

CONSIDERING AUTOTRADED ASSET REVESTING

Autotraded asset revesting allows you to have a specific strategy followed and positions executed in your account while you're busy working, running your business, or spending time with family and friends. In short, it allows you to have your account actively managed to protect against market declines, and it can generate gains on autopilot during bear markets. There are two ways to have asset revesting signals autotraded. First, you can find a newsletter that provides the signals and has partnered with a brokerage to have autotrading as an option. Or you can work with your financial advisor to add these signals to the accounts you are already paying them to manage.

IS AUTOMATED ASSET REVESTING RISKY?

Autotrading within an account is no riskier than the strategy that serves as the foundation for the automation. In the past few years, millions of investors have chosen to have their portfolios autotraded by robo-advisors. These services offer lower cost investing than traditional advisor services offered by firms like Fidelity and Schwab. While advisors in general focus on traditional higher-risk strategies, such as buy-and-hold, diversification, dividend reinvesting, etc., autotrading an asset revesting strategy can avoid common risks associated with holding a basket of investments that are falling in value.

As you have already read so far, if you compare traditional investment methods to an asset revesting strategy, the difference in risk is fairly large.

ADVANTAGES OF AUTOMATED INVESTING SYSTEMS

- **Consistency**: One of the biggest challenges in trading is to plan the trade and trade the plan. Even if a trading plan has the potential to be profitable, traders who ignore the rules are altering any expectancy the system would have had. Losing trades can be psychologically traumatizing, so a trader who has two or three losing trades in a row might decide to skip the next one. But the reality is, when a strategy falls out of favor temporarily and has a few losing trades, and then the market turns more favorable for the strategy, the next trade or two can produce oversized returns. These are important trades you can't afford to miss. Having a strategy autotraded allows you to achieve more consistent results. As explained earlier in the wealth math section, consistency is the key to a great retirement lifestyle.

- **Reduce order entry delays**: Since computers can respond instantly, automated systems are able to trigger orders as soon as a set of trade rules is met. Getting in or out of a trade a few hours earlier can make a big difference in the trade's outcome. This is especially true over many years when dozens of trades have been taken.

- **Minimize emotions**: Having your investment capital managed for you can reduce your emotions and help you stick to your strategy. With the trades executed automatically, you won't be able to hesitate or skip a trade. If you're afraid to pull the trigger or more apt to overtrade, you will benefit greatly from automated execution.

- **Preserve discipline**: In most cases, discipline is lost due to the fear and greed factor. The fear of taking a loss or the desire to squeeze out a little more profit from a trade hurts discipline. With trading rules already established and trade execution performed automatically, discipline is preserved even during volatile market conditions. Pilot error is also minimized.

HOW AUTOMATION NARROWS INVESTING'S GENDER GAP

When traveling by rail in the UK, passengers are frequently told to "mind the gap." This reminder warns riders about the space between the station platform and the railcar. A similar warning should be issued to women who are facing the prospect of investing their savings.

As in many areas of our society, there is a gender gap in investing, and it rarely favors women.

According to a survey by NerdWallet, fewer women than men have learned about investing, invest their own savings, and feel secure about making investment decisions.[8] In fact, the prevalent emotion women feel when thinking about investing is anxiety.

---

8   El Issa, E. Survey: Less Than Half of Women in U.S. Invest in the Stock Market. *Nerdwallet*. September 1, 2021. Accessed July 19, 2023. https://www.nerdwallet.com/article/investing/survey-less-than-half-of-   women-in-u-s-invest-in-the-stock-market.

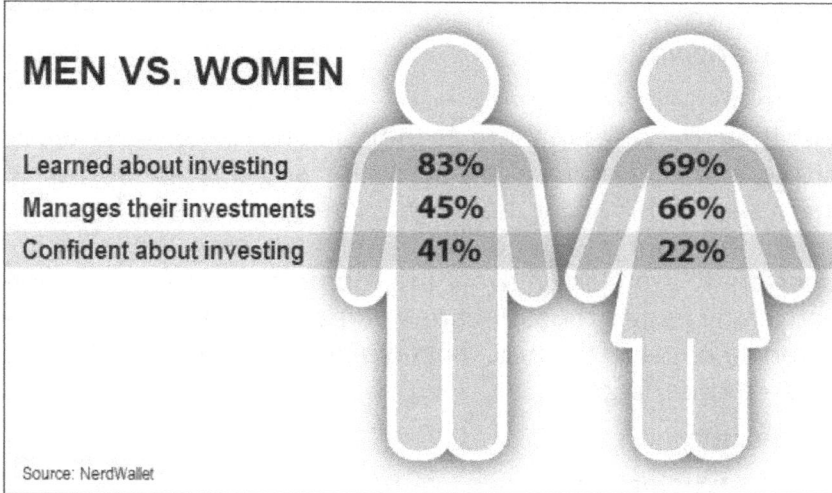

MEN VS. WOMEN		
Learned about investing	83%	69%
Manages their investments	45%	66%
Confident about investing	41%	22%

Source: NerdWallet

Figure 23

Women are already facing a lifetime income gap of $80,000.[9] Worse, poverty rates for women are higher.[10] With all this working against women, isn't it time there was something that works for them? Asset revesting through autotrading may be the answer.

PRIORITIZING WHAT WOMEN WANT

While over 50 percent of women handle their household finances today, they are still more likely to turn to an outside advisor to handle their investments.[11] Yet, finding the right advisor isn't simple. Just ask the more than 80 percent of

---

9   Marquit, M. Women and Investing: The Surprising Statistics You Should Know [2023]. *FinanceBuzz*. April 3, 2023. Accessed July 19, 2023. https://financebuzz.com/women-and-investing-statistics.
10   American Progress. The Basic Facts About Women in Poverty. *American Progress*. August 3, 2020. Accessed July 19, 2023. https://www.americanprogress.org/article/basic-facts-women-poverty/.
11   Settembre, J. Women Are Calling the Shots When It Comes to Household Finances. *Marketwatch*. March 19, 2018. Accessed July 19, 2023. https://www.marketwatch.com/story/women-are-calling-the-shots-   when-it-comes-to-household-finances-2018-03-19-7885731.

widows who leave the advisor their spouse worked with and find their own.[12]

One of the reasons many women leave financial advisors is that they feel disrespected as their unique investment needs are ignored. Therefore, a priority for any advisor or investment research service helping women invest is to focus on what they want and need that differs from men. While it's impossible to state definitively the top priorities for every person in any large group, decades of research have shown that when it comes to finance, most women are concerned about these three things:[13]

- Security
- Lifestyle maintenance
- Poor market performance

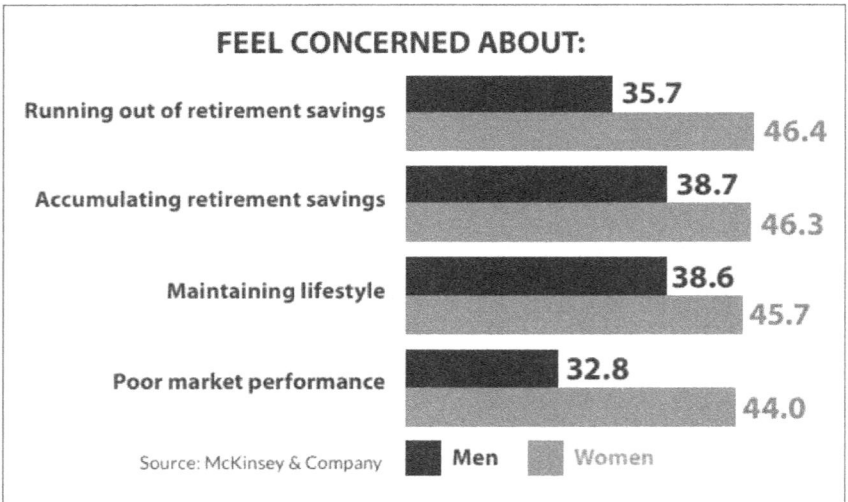

Figure 24

12   Francis, S. Widows Move Forward on Their Own – But Not Alone. *Kiplinger.* May 30, 2021. Accessed July 19, 2023. https://www.kiplinger.com/personal-finance/602892/widows-move-for- ward-on-their-own-but-not-alone.

13   Baghai, P., et al. Women as the next wave of growth in US wealth management. *McKinsey.* July 29, 2020. Accessed July 19, 2023. https://www.mckinsey.com/industries/financial-services/our-insights/   women-as-the-next-wave-of-growth-in-us-wealth-management.

UNDERSTANDING WHAT WOMEN NEED

Recent research has shown us that women need less stress. They routinely take on more of the housework and childcare duties in a family, even spending more of their leisure time providing care for children or parents instead of trying to relax or engage in their hobbies.

Many of them simply don't have the time or emotional energy to constantly monitor the performance of their portfolio and make ongoing tactical decisions.

This often leads to buy-and-hold positions. In fact, Vanguard recently found that women are 50 percent less likely to trade actively. Sadly, this does nothing to minimize investing's gender gap.

Investing in positions over the long term and avoiding active management of your portfolio to allow the market to "do its thing" can work, especially during a bull market and if you are far enough away from retirement. But with increasing volatility and more frequent market downturns, buy-and-hold/hope is a risky way to invest your life savings.

MEETING WOMEN'S EXPECTATIONS

When it comes to investing, women often lack confidence. Only 33 percent surveyed by Fidelity would even consider calling themselves investors, and just 35 percent are confident that their savings are appropriately invested.

Financial literacy is definitely part of the problem, as only 14 percent of surveyed women said they had a large amount of knowledge about saving and investing. Increasing financial literacy is a great way to combat this—but how much money is being lost right now by women who are hesitant to start investing until they "catch up"?

The answer to narrowing this gap might be found with the automated asset revesting system offered by some financial newsletters. Not only does this option resolve many of the specific concerns and obstacles facing women who want to invest, but it also ensures that they have the level footing necessary to help break through investing's glass ceiling and get more reliable results. If you're a woman, this can allow you to catch up on lost time and avoid using an underper-forming investment strategy.

CHAPTER 8:
THE PRICE OF INVESTING

Investment results are one way to measure the financial firm, advisor, research, and automation service you want to handle your investing. The second way is by reviewing the cost of each investment option. Also in the mix are the various investment requirements that must be met to qualify. Let's take a look at some of the most popular investment advice, research options, and automated investing services. We will look at each one's investing style, cost, and required minimum investments so that you can decide which one is best for you. Let's kick it off with hedge funds.

HEDGE FUND

- **Investing style**: Hedge funds follow their individual strategy rules and hold specific positions and/or follow a strategy, no matter if it works in the current market condition. This can lead to severe losses.

- **Costs**: Management fees of up to 2 percent and performance bonuses of up to 20 percent of the total profit.

- **Required minimums**: Minimum investment of at least $100,000.[14] Must be an accredited investor with net worth of $1 million or annual income over $200,000.

- **Comments**: The average hedge fund underperforms the SP500 benchmark. We hear about hedge funds blowing up all the time when there is a strong market correction.

FINANCIAL ADVISOR

- **Investing style**: Depends on both investor and advisor. Investors are part of the decision-making process, but most advisors base their solutions around the traditional diversified buy-and-hold portfolio.

- **Costs**: Management fees range (on average) from 1 percent to 1.5 percent.

- Required minimums: Generally at least $50,000. Some may require as much as $1,000,000.[15]

- **Comments**: While financial advisors can offer personalized guidance, many charge a high fee based on assets under management (AUM), which may erode long-term returns. Additionally, studies have shown that many advisors consistently underperform the market and lack downside protection.

ROBO-ADVISOR

- **Investing style**: Varies depending on your style and risk tolerance. Algorithms determine investment activities.

- **Costs**: Varies—anywhere from 0.25 percent to 0.89 percent. Some include annual fees and setup fees as well.

- **Required minimums**: Varies—anywhere from $0 to $100,000.

---

14   Cautero, R. How a Separately Managed Account (SMA) Works. SmartAsset. April 1, 2022. Accessed July 19, 2023. https://smartasset.com/investing/separately-managed-account.

15   John Hancock. What is a separately managed account? John Hancock. July 5, 2023. Accessed July 19, 2023. https://www. jhinvestments.com/viewpoints/investing-basics/ what-are-separately-managed-accounts.

- **Comments**: Sadly, robo-advisors, which were created to help reduce the AUM cost of investors, seem to be primarily focused on the same old approaches, including buy-and-hold, diversification, and dividend reinvestment. That means many of them don't have the programming to recognize the signals necessary to create an asset revesting portfolio. Therefore, they miss out on capturing the additional gains created by market volatility and bear markets. The Robo Report shows that during the five-year window from 2017 to 2022, returns on investment from traditional robo-advisors have been poor with an average range of only 2 percent to 5 percent per year.

ASSET REVESTING

- **Investing style**: Uses a proven alternative investment strategy that focuses on portfolio preservation and risk management. Exclusively invests in and holds assets that are rising in value by following the trends of assets using technical analysis.

- **Costs**: Low flat annual subscription fee. (*If you already have money with an advisor, then you may be able to have asset revesting signals autotraded for you at no additional cost.*)

- **Required minimums**: None.

- **Comments**: Takes part in market rallies; avoids or profits from declining prices with noncorrelated assets. Allows autotrading for a total solution for investors; investment capital autotraded in a self-directed investment account at no additional fee/cost or manually trade the detailed newsletter signals yourself. The chart in figure 25 is an example using a moderately priced fee for an asset revesting newsletter subscription.

ASSETS		BUY-AND-HOLD INVESTING			CGS REVESTING	
Portfolio Size	**Fee**	**Advisor AUM Cost**			**Cost**	
$50K - $1M	1.20%	Up to $12,000	**Avg. Annual Return** 7.72%		$2,499	**Avg. Annual Return** 15.62%
$1M - $3M	1.00%	$12,000 - $32,000			$2,499	
$3M -$7M	0.80%	$32,000 - $64,000			$2,499	
$7M -$15M	0.65%	$64,000 - $116,000			$2,499	

Figure 25

INDIVIDUAL INVESTOR (SELF-MANAGED)

- **Investing style**: Self-determined and maintained. Methods are generally discretionary, driven by emotional impulse, and will lack proper position and risk management processes.

- **Costs**: Individual commissions for trades and account fees depend on brokerage.

- **Required minimums**: None.

- **Comments**: Subject to 50+ percent drawdowns, overtrading, and poor market timing, leading to increased losses. Stressful to manage and difficult to invest and generate consistent returns during bull and bear markets.

Every investor is different, and your needs won't be quite like anyone else's. Still, when you consider the costs, the range of investing styles, and the various minimum requirements, following asset revesting signals from a newsletter and/or having asset revesting signals autotraded offer some of the most efficient and cost-effective ways to have capital actively managed and protected.

EXPLORING ADVISORLESS ASSET REVESTING

Not every investor wants to work with an advisor. The commissions, meetings, potential conflicts of interest, and lack of fiduciary requirements can be a real obstacle for investors who have observed shifts in the financial industry since the 2008 financial crisis and 2022. If that's you, advisorless asset revesting may be the ideal choice.

Advisorless asset revesting involves the self-management or autotraded signals of your investment account. In this scenario, you either manually manage your own position, based on signals for various assets in a hierarchy, or you have assets autotraded for you. This includes moving capital out of falling investments and into rising investments, as well as setting and recalculating protective stops and selling positions to reduce risk and exposure when certain profit target levels have been reached.

PRIMARY BENEFITS OF ADVISORLESS REVESTING

There are powerful benefits to advisorless revesting, but the main ones are:

1. **Lower costs**. One of the biggest benefits of advisorless revesting is that it's generally less expensive than working with traditional financial firms that charge 1 percent AUM fees. Without the need to pay for an advisor, you can keep more of your money working for you. Saving 1 percent per year allows for additional compounding, which helps you retire with quite a bit more money.

2. **Convenience**. Advisorless revesting offers greater convenience, as you can manage your investments online without scheduling calls and meetings with an advisor to do paperwork.

3. **Control**. Advisorless revesting provides you with more control over your capital. You can change your portfolio positions as you see fit, rather than relying on an advisor to decide for you.

4. **Automated trading**. Those who are dissatisfied with the limitations of a traditional buy-and-hold investing method now have access to automated trading systems. Autotrading can reduce costs and make it simple for you to have your money managed for you.

5. **Investors currently using an advisor**. Can have both asset revesting signals and autotrading working for them

at no additional cost to what they pay with their advisor. In fact, we find most clients save $5,000 to $30,000 per year by making the switch with some of or all of their investment account.

10 YEAR APPLES-TO-APPLES COMPARISON: ASSET REVESTING VERSUS BUY-AND-HOLD

As mentioned in earlier chapters, withdrawing funds when a portfolio is in a drawdown can be very costly to your long-term financial outlook. But with a tactical investing strategy like revesting, you shouldn't have any big losses or multi-year periods of negative returns. That means a portfolio will generally be near a high watermark (all-time high), leaving you free to withdraw capital as needed and continue to grow your wealth while in retirement.

Please note that in the following example, I have used my own asset revesting strategy as an example (as I did in Figure 15). This is not done to entice you to my company but rather to illustrate a point in the best way that I can do so. As you can see in Figure 26, the lifestyle of a retiree withdrawing $50,000 a year that manages risk vs. a retiree who does nothing is dramatically different. The revester becomes wealthier, while the traditional investor treads water and falls behind when we account for inflation.

Year	Withdrawal	Return	Y/E Value	Year	Withdrawal	Return	Y/E Value
Starting Capital: $1,000,000 Multi Assset Revesting - CGS Strategy				Starting Capital: $1,000,000 Buy-and-Hold 60/40 Strategy			
2013	$50,000	11.48%	$1,059,060	2013	$50,000	13.70%	$1,080,150
2014	$50,000	19.61%	$1,206,937	2014	$50,000	5.40%	$1,085,778
2015	$50,000	8.18%	$1,255,664	2015	$50,000	-1.40%	$1,021,277
2016	$50,000	8.31%	$1,310,010	2016	$50,000	6.80%	$1,037,324
2017	$50,000	15.67%	$1,465,288	2017	$50,000	15.60%	$1,141,347
2018	$50,000	7.95%	$1,531,779	2018	$50,000	-5.40%	$1,032,414
2019	$50,000	13.93%	$1,695,155	2019	$50,000	19.10%	$1,170,055
2020	$50,000	52.81%	$2,540,367	2020	$50,000	13.00%	$1,265,662
2021	$50,000	16.84%	$2,918,165	2021	$50,000	10.10%	$1,338,444
2022	$50,000	5.49%	$3,028,372	2022	$50,000	-19.11%	$1,042,222
AVERAGE RETURN		16.03%		AVERAGE RETURN		5.78%	

Figure 26

While there is no guarantee that investments will always yield positive results, a well-managed portfolio will likely have more consistently positive results than negative ones. It's important to understand that results don't come in a linear fashion. Just like flying an airplane across the country, it isn't as simple as going in a straight line because, with the winds aloft, the shape of the earth, and its rotation, a straight-line approach won't get you where you want to go.

Asset revesting provides both consistency and a higher average annual return, which supercharges our investment accounts. Investors who can change course as needed with their investments are able to continue building their wealth and improving their lifestyle.

Each individual or company that provides this unique investment style will have their own asset hierarchy and trading rules they follow. Don't be surprised when others haven't heard about it because the financial industry and advisors don't embrace this type of investing, yet.

CONCLUSION

Ever since I began trading, I've become more and more passionate about helping others increase their skills and investment returns. My excitement for investing continues to grow each year, and I suspect it'll be the same for you. Once you have some wealth accumulated, the gains compound quickly, and it's addicting and rewarding like no other business.

I've worked hard to research the markets. I have lived and breathed trading since I was sixteen years old, and I'm now in my forties. I have survived and thrived through many bear markets, corrections, and wild market-moving events, and I want to give you the most current understanding of the financial market as a whole. Asset revesting has been key, and it provides a clear and simple solution for any trader.

As an investor, your ultimate goal should be to think of yourself as a risk manager. Continually reassess risk, and adjust your profit targets and protective stops. Always know what you're going to do before you do it. This will keep emotion from creeping in, which will steal or limit profits, break your trading rules, and undermine all your hard work. If you can manage risk, and therefore your emotions, the profits will follow.

In markets like those we have today, a trader's top priority is protecting capital. The reality is that it's extremely difficult to survive a bear market unscathed—unless you have proper guidance. If you don't have the guidance, you're probably going to face some deep financial trouble. You may have to delay your retirement or worse—completely shelve the idea of retirement altogether.

These risks are the whole reason why I'm committed to helping you learn how to take advantage of falling prices and advantage of new bull markets when they happen. So many people think avoiding corrections and bear markets is difficult. They think the markets can't be navigated. They've been brainwashed into believing that the traditional methods are the only way to lock in long-term gains. My experience and that of countless others has proven otherwise, which I've shown throughout this book.

This book, however, is just one piece of the process. You are now aware that there is a *different* way to invest and protect your capital. You now have investment options to choose from so that you can reach retirement sooner or generate more income in retirement.

If you follow the rules and tips for asset revesting contained within these pages, you will be off to a great start to creating your own asset hierarchy and strategy that fits your personality, risk, and available time. Or you will feel more confident about having one executed for you. Then, just maybe when the next downturn happens (and they always happen), you will be sitting on the sidelines toasting your good fortune with the cash you would have lost had you not found asset revesting.

Ask yourself the following questions:

- Are you sick of watching your investments lose value?
- Does losing significant amounts of your portfolio keep you up at night?
- Does the stress of investing your money make you miserable and sick, but you don't want to pay an advisor?
- Are you ready to overcome investment fears to create a better future for yourself and your family?

Notice that every single one of these questions is under your control to change!

Asset Revesting is simply the first step.

No more emotions in the way, no more switching and jumping from one strategy to another, no more aggressive trading that leads to big losses, no more struggling to follow a clear trading plan. Instead:

You can generate higher returns worry-free.

Your retirement can grow continuously with minimal effort and without drawdowns.

You can spend more time doing the things you enjoy, including hobbies and travel, without worrying about money.

You can enjoy your family and friends more.

You can prudently conserve and grow wealth as a legacy for your family and the charities of your choice.

But don't take my word for it. Listen to people who have already taken the plunge, taken control, and who opted to use my asset revesting signals service:

"This service is a calm in the storm with regards to this crazy market. It is helping me grow and protect my retirement savings through use of a controlled complex system which is quite easy to use." Ron Smith

"Chris gives daily video updates and really helps me to understand the markets and control my emotions when investing and trading. My results are now consistent, and I am making of my investments." Richard Jaques

"Every morning, you get an 8-12 minutes video explaining the market conditions and what to expect in the market. Then at the end of the trading day he sends out another afternoon update summarizing the market and reviewing the trades. Customer service is exceptional. I have often emailed them with questions and received a reply the same day." Steve Sohm

"I am an industry professional of 30+ years and have worked in London for all that time. Seldom (if ever) have I felt so relaxed about leaning on technical analysis. My aim is to 'lean' more and more on this excellent service!" Jonathan Morgan

Become a revester, and join the thousands people like you experiencing more consistent returns and a richer, happier live.

FREE GOODWILL

"He who said money can't buy happiness, hasn't given enough money away."
- Unknown

Did you know that people who help others with zero expectation of reciprocal behaviour experience higher levels of fulfillment in life, love, longevity, and prosperity?

I'd like to provide an opportunity for free goodwill during your reading experience. To do so, I have a simple question for you:

Would you help someone you've never met if it didn't cost you money, and you never got credit for it?

If so, I have an "ask" to make on behalf of someone you do not know well, and likely, will never meet in person.

They are just like you, or like how you were years ago: less experienced, full of desire to help others, seeking information, but unsure where to look. This is where you come in.

The only way for us at TheTechnicalTraders.com to accomplish our mission of helping entrepreneurs, professionals, traders, and investors is by reaching them. Most people do, in fact, judge a book by its cover and its reviews. If you have found this book valuable thus far, would you please take a moment right now and leave an honest review of the book and its contents? It will cost you zero dollars and take less than 90 seconds.

Your review will help:

. . . one more employee reach retirement sooner.

. . . one more busy professional to invest better and support their family.

. . . one more investor experience a transformation and leave a legacy they never knew possible.

. . . secure one more retiree's income and lifestyle.

To make this happen... all you have to do is to leave a review.

<u>If you are reading on Kindle or an E-reader,</u> you can swipe up, and it will automatically prompt a review.

<u>If you bought paperback or hardcover,</u> you can go to the book page on Amazon (or wherever you made the purchase) and leave a review on the page.

From the bottom of my heart, thank you for your consideration!

Your biggest fan, Chris

PS: If you feel good about helping others, you are my kind of person! I'm both excited and honoured to help you learn about a different way to gain control and become financially free in the coming chapters. You'll love learning about this investing style.

PPS — Bonus Goodwill: If you introduce something valuable to someone you know, they will associate that value with you forever. If you'd like to cast a wide net of goodwill and inspire others to do the same, send this book their way.

ABOUT THE AUTHOR

Chief Investment Officer Chris Vermeulen has spent more than twenty-five years as a technical analyst, equities trader, investment strategist, thought leader, educator, and entrepreneur.

His extensive trading and investment background comes from devoting his life to studying the financial markets, technical analysis, and risk management. Having traded and invested through multiple bull and bear market cycles, Chris understands the importance of capital preservation.

He is also the author of *Technical Trading Mastery — 7 Steps To Win With Logic,* which is the prequel to *Asset Revesting.* He has been a guest on numerous financial sites and stations, including Sprott Money, Cheddar, Yahoo Finance, Kitco, David Lin Report, and many others.

ABOUT THE CO-AUTHOR

Ashley Mulock, Chief Operating Officer at The Technical Traders, brings a unique and diverse background, honing communication and logistical skills across multiple fields after degrees in Outdoor Recreation, Tourism, and Geography.

With a Business Certificate and a degree from The University of Life, Ashley offers a fresh perspective, focusing on Operations, Client Care, and Finance.

As a student of trading and investing, Ashley naturally gravitated toward lower-risk investing strategies, which made logical sense, only to find out later that the investment industry uses risky methods. So after collaborating with others, she helped cocreate Asset Revesting, a style of investing that protects capital during volatile market conditions while generating solid returns for investors without risking their retirement.

TRADING RESOURCES

Technical Trading Mastery – 2nd Edition

Recommended reading for creating an asset reinvesting strategy: "7 Steps to Win with Logic" offers a proven foundation. The author Chris Vermeulen shares twenty-plus years of successful trading experience and detailed strategies to follow.

www.TheTechnicalTraders.com/books

Asset Revesting

Imagine if you could sell your investments as they started to top, then revest your money into different assets rising in value and never have to hold falling positions again.

www.Revesting.com

The Technical Traders

Asset revesting strategies, automated investing, educational videos, articles, and market commentary.

www.TheTechnicalTraders.com

*THANK YOU
GIFT VALUED AT $249*

QUARTERLY INVESTOR TREND REPORT

Be on the right side of the stock market. Own only assets rising in value. Retire sooner and wealthier.

Everything you learned in this book has been applied to the stock market and summarized for your convenience in the Quarterly Investor Trend Report. You will know what to expect regarding market stages and volatility and receive my market trend stage gauge to visually see where the market is and where it is likely headed.

FREE MEMBERSHIP FOR LIFE – LIMITED OFFER

Name: _____

Email: _____

SUBMIT

Visit: www.AssetRevesting.com

www.ingramcontent.com/pod-product-compliance
Lightning Source LLC
Chambersburg PA
CBHW030529210326
41597CB00013B/1080